Children's
Great Explorers
Encyclopedia

Author: Simon Adams

Consultant: Philip Parker

This edition produced by Tall Tree Ltd, London

First published by Parragon in 2008
Parragon
Queen Street House
4 Queen Street
Bath BA1 1HE, UK

ISBN 978-1-4075-0321-9

Printed in Malaysia

Children's Great Explorers Encyclopedia

Discover the world in the footsteps of famous explorers

Simon Adams

PaRRagon

Bath New York Singapore Hong Kong Cologne Delhi Melbourne

Greenland

Hudson
Bay

Labrador
Sea

North
America

Atlantic Ocean

N
NW   NE
W   E
SW
SE
S

CONTENTS

INTRODUCTION

Human beings once lived only in East Africa. People first left this region about 50,000 years ago, and ever since we have been driven by the urge to explore. Brave explorers have pushed back the frontiers and reached the most hostile places on the Earth. Every continent has been explored, from the tropical jungles to the icy poles, and many people have lost their lives in the process. Recently, we have even begun to discover what lies beyond our planet. Here we tell the stories of some extraordinary explorers, from the first journeys ever recorded to modern-day adventurers. These are the explorations that have shaped the world we know today.

EARLY EXPLORERS

The first travellers all set out on their journeys for a reason. The Egyptians, Phoenicians and Greeks travelled for trade. The Chinese left home to find new allies or to seek out the teachings of Buddha. The Norsemen set sail in search of new places to live. We know about these early adventurers because some of them wrote about their journeys, which took them to the very edges of their known world.

Voyage to Punt

We do not know the name of the first explorer. However, we do know that the Ancient Egyptians undertook a voyage to a place called Punt about 3500 years ago, during the reign of Queen Hatshepsut.

By land and sea

After making contact with the people of Punt, the Egyptians travelled there in order to trade. We do not know where Punt was, but it may have been in northern Somalia, at the end of the Red Sea. The Egyptians dragged all the materials they needed to build their ships overland from the River Nile to the Red Sea coast. There they built five ships and sailed south for a year.

Queen Hatshepsut

Hatshepsut ruled Egypt from around 1473–1458 BC. She was often portrayed in statues as a man. This is because it was almost unheard of at the time for a woman to become a pharaoh (Egyptian ruler).

Hatshepsut's temple

Hatshepsut built a huge temple in which to protect her body when she died. The temple is built into cliffs on the west bank of the River Nile at Thebes, one of the main religious centres of Egypt.

Carvings on the temple walls tell us about the voyage to Punt.

The riches of Punt

Once in Punt, the Egyptians loaded their ships with myrrh trees, incense, ivory, ebony, gold, leopard skins and other luxuries. They also took live animals with them, such as baboons and pet dogs. Once their ships were full, they sailed north again up the Red Sea. They crossed over land once more to the River Nile and sailed home.

Hatshepsut's temple walls depict the triumphant return of the sailors from Punt.

Timeline

c.2500 BC
Ancient Egyptians first make contact with Punt

c.1473
Hatshepsut rules on behalf of her infant stepson Thutmose III

c.1470
Hatshepsut orders the voyage to Punt to bring back precious items for her temples and palaces

c.1458
Hatshepsut dies

It's Amazing!

An inscription in the temple states that "Never was the like brought to any monarch since the world began".

Egyptian ships

The trading ships of Ancient Egypt were made of short planks of wood tied together with rope around a basic wooden frame. The ships had one large linen sail and up to 16 oars on either side to propel them when the wind was light or in the wrong direction. A large oar at the back was used for steering.

The trading ships had plenty of room inside to store the items traded in Punt.

Phoenician traders

The Phoenicians, a people from Lebanon, on the east coast of the Mediterranean Sea, established colonies where they could trade with the local people. One of these colonies was Carthage in North Africa.

The voyage of Hanno

Around 475 BC, one trader, Hanno, led a fleet of 60 ships out of Carthage to search for new places to establish colonies. They sailed out of the Mediterranean and down the coast of Africa. Along the way they saw a volcano erupting. They may have sailed as far as Mt Cameroon, which is the only volcano on the west coast.

It's Amazing!

Hanno records meeting people covered with hair, whom he called 'Gorillas'.

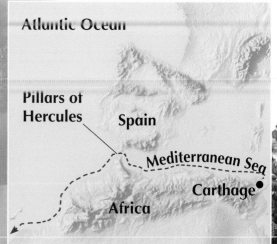

The Pillars of Hercules marked the end of the known world.

Pillars of Hercules

As Hanno and his fleet headed west, they passed between the Pillars of Hercules. These two rocks are thought to have been the Rock of Gibraltar on the European coast and Mt Hacho on the African coast.

Phoenician ships may have looked like this.

Phoenician ships

We don't know much about Phoenician trading ships as records about them lack any technical details. They were probably made of wood planks and powered with a single sail and rows of oars on either side.

The colour purple

The Phoenicians were famous for their fine purple cloth. They extracted a liquid from sea snails to make the dye. Up to 30,000 snails were needed for each kilogram of dye, so purple cloth was very expensive.

Purple cloth was so rare that it was only worn by the very rich.

These ruins in present-day Tunisia are almost all that is left of the great city of Carthage.

Timeline

c.814 BC
Phoenicians establish trading city Carthage in North Africa

c.600 BC
A Phoenician ship sails around Africa

c.475 BC
Hanno sails down the west coast of Africa

Round Africa

Hanno was not the first Phoenician traveller. In around 600 BC, the Egyptian pharaoh Necho II hired a Phoenician crew to sail down the Red Sea, around Africa and then back through the Mediterranean to Egypt. The voyage took three years because the crew stopped each year to plant and reap a harvest of food.

Around Britain

The Ancient Greeks were great traders and explorers. In 330 BC a Greek merchant, Pytheas, made one of the most remarkable voyages of the ancient world.

Pytheas

Pytheas was born around 380 BC in Massilia, a Greek colony in southern France, known today as Marseilles. During his voyage, he was the first to describe the aurora borealis, or northern lights, the glowing green sky that sometimes occurs in the far north.

It's Amazing!

Tin from Cornwall was taken at low tide to the island of St Michael's Mount. The merchants who bought it were scared to go to the mainland because the locals were so fierce!

To Thule

Pytheas set out from Massilia through the Mediterranean. He followed the Atlantic coastline north until he crossed the English Channel to Cornwall. Here he saw mines extracting and refining tin into fist-sized ingots. He then sailed north up the Irish Sea and through the Hebrides to the Orkney Islands at the top of Scotland. From here he sailed north for a further six days until he sighted Thule, "the most distant of all the lands".

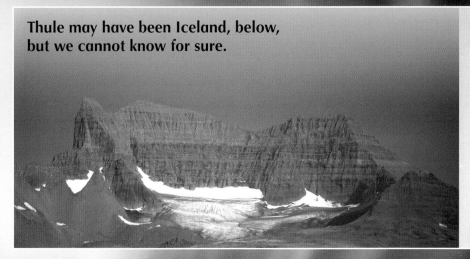

Thule may have been Iceland, below, but we cannot know for sure.

Thule

We do not know where Thule was, but Pytheas said that the Sun never set there and the sea was transformed into a material "on which it was neither possible to walk nor to sail" – ice. This suggests Thule was close to the Arctic Ocean.

The spectacular northern lights were observed by Pytheas at Thule.

The Greeks made goods to trade, such as this necklace.

Greek trade

The Ancient Greeks founded many colonies around the Mediterranean and Black seas. These colonies grew rich by trading tin, grain and other raw materials in return for Greek goods such as wine and jewellery.

Homeward bound

At Thule, Pytheas turned back south, exploring the east coast of Britain and then crossing the North Sea to the Amber Islands off the coast of Denmark. From there he returned to Massilia, probably by sailing up the River Rhine and then travelling across land to sail down the River Rhone to the coast.

In defence of China

In 138 BC, the Chinese empire was under threat from the Huns, a nomadic tribe from central Asia. In response, the Chinese emperor Wudi sent one of his officials to seek allies among neighbouring states.

The futile search

Zhang Qian set out from the Chinese capital, Chang'an, with a plan to enlist the help of the Yue-chi tribe of central Asia. But before reaching them, he was captured by the Huns and imprisoned for 10 years. When he finally escaped, he travelled east to Ferghana, where he met the Yue-chi. However, they refused to fight the Huns, so Zhang Qian returned home empty-handed.

Timeline

c.160 BC
Birth of Zhang Qian

138–127 BC
Zhang Qian seeks an alliance with the Yue-chi but is imprisoned by the Huns

126 BC
Zhang returns home

119 BC
Zhang's second journey to central Asia

107 BC
Zhang Qian dies

c.100 BC
The Silk Road opens

Black Sea

Caspian Sea

Ferghana

Kashgar

Antioch

Merv

Khotan

Ecbatana

Gaofucheng

P A R T H I A

━━━━━ The main Silk Road

╍╍╍╍ First journey

╍╍╍╍ Second journey

I N D I A

Red Sea

Arabian Sea

Han Dynasty

The Han Dynasty of emperors ruled China from 206 BC until AD 220. The emperors believed their great power came from heaven. They governed the country through a series of powerful land-owning families. They also built up a large army and extended their empire to cover much of modern-day China.

The Han made sophisticated ceramics, such as this one of a much-prized Ferghana horse.

Longcheng

Gobi Desert

Dunhuang

C H I N A

Tarim Basin

Chang'an

Opening up the west

The emperor was very interested in Zhang Qian's reports of the people who lived to the west of his borders. Around 116 BC, Wudi sent Zhang Qian back to meet these people again. This time he had more success. He made useful contacts and explored the trade routes that linked China with Kashgar and Ferghana, and south into India.

What Next?

Zhang Qian's report to the emperor led to the opening of the Silk Road, a new trade route to Parthia and the Roman empire. The Silk Road remained the main trade route between China and Europe for many centuries.

In search of Buddha

Buddhism reached China from India in about AD 70, but contact between the two countries was restricted by the Himalaya Mountains that separated them. Two Chinese monks travelled to India to find out more about their religion.

Faxian the monk

In AD 399 Faxian set out from China and travelled west along the Silk Road to Khotan in the far west, where he found many Buddhist monks. He then headed south across the mountains into India where he studied in the Buddhist monasteries along the River Ganges. After further stops in Sri Lanka, Malaya and Indonesia, he returned home in AD 412 with manuscripts and sacred objects.

There are many giant statues of Buddha like this one in south Asia.

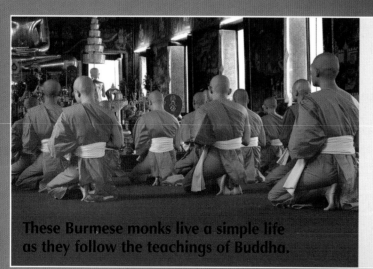

These Burmese monks live a simple life as they follow the teachings of Buddha.

Buddhism

Buddha was born in northern India in 485 BC. He taught that people could overcome suffering and hardship in the world by becoming enlightened and reaching a state of supreme happiness. From India, Buddhism spread into Tibet, China, Korea and Japan, and south to Sri Lanka and southeast Asia.

Timeline

c. AD 337
Birth of Faxian

AD 399–412
Faxian travels to India

AD 422
Death of Faxian

c. AD 602
Xuanzang born

AD 629–45
Xuanzang travels to India via central Asia

AD 664
Xuanzang dies

Xuanzang

Xuanzang was born in AD 602 and left for India when he was 27. He was anxious to explain the difficult teachings he found in Buddhist texts. By the time he returned home, 16 years later, he had collected over 650 religious books.

Xuanzang carried his books on his back.

The ancient scholar

In AD 629, the monk Xuanzang set out to India to study the old Buddhist texts. He learned the ancient Indian language of Sanskrit and travelled round the country, finding out about Buddha and his teachings. His journal describes the approximately 60,000 kilometres he travelled. It became an important source of information on the geography of India and China.

What Next?

The Chinese invented a method of printing blocks of text onto paper around the AD 500s so that more people could read the new Buddhist texts.

Man of letters

Faxian's name means "Illustrious master of the Law", for he was a brilliant Buddhist scholar. We know little about his life other than what he recorded in his book, *A Record of Buddhistic Kingdoms*.

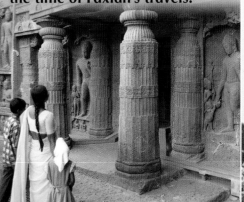

The Ajanta monastery in India was carved out of rock around the time of Faxian's travels.

The Norsemen

We often think of the Norsemen, or Vikings, as savage raiders, looting and pillaging. But the Norsemen were also intrepid travellers and traders. They were the first Europeans to visit North America.

Leif Erikson

Around AD 1000, Leif Erikson visited North America, sailing from Greenland down the coast of Labrador. He reached a place he named Vinland (Wine-land) because of its wild berries.

Setting sail

We are not sure why in the 9th century AD the Norsemen decided to leave home. However, it is likely that the growing number of younger sons with no land to inherit drove many to seek their fortune abroad. Their boats loaded up with provisions, they set out across the Atlantic Ocean.

Viking ships set sail in search of adventure and new lands.

Timeline

Norse navigation

The Norsemen found their way across the oceans using the Sun and stars. By lining up a wooden bearing dial with the Sun at noon, they could determine which direction was south.

One of the notches on this bearing dial points south at noon.

New world

The first Norse settlements were established in Ireland, the isles of Scotland and the Faeroe Islands. By AD 870 the Norsemen had settled in Iceland. A century later, Erik the Red ventured across to Greenland, then much warmer than it is today. In AD 1000 the Norse leader Leif Erikson reached as far as Newfoundland, in Canada, and possibly further. A later attempt to settle the region by Thorfinn Karlsefni was unsuccessful and the Norsemen soon forgot about this new world.

What Next?

By the 1400s the climate of Greenland had become much colder, so the Vikings abandoned their settlements, leaving the island to its original Inuit inhabitants.

Settling the new land

In 1960 a Norwegian archaeologist, Helge Ingstad, discovered the foundation posts of two Norse houses at L'Anse aux Meadows, on the northern tip of Newfoundland, Canada. These houses may be the Vinland settlement, although some historians think Vinland was further down the coast, perhaps near Cape Cod.

A reconstruction of the Norse settlement at L'Anse aux Meadows.

A Viking voyage

The Vikings, or Norsemen, who sailed west from Norway across the North Atlantic Ocean were skilled and brave seafarers, risking their lives in open boats to search for new lands. Most could not read or write, so they passed on their stories by word of mouth. Many of these stories were later written down in the great Norse sagas. This is a fictional diary of a voyage along the main route to Greenland.

GREENLAND

ICELAND

FAEROE ISLANDS

NORWAY

Hvarf

Bergen

Herjolfsnes

SHETLAND ISLANDS

ATLANTIC OCEAN

EUROPE

Due West

With great sadness I left my home in Bergen seven days ago bound for Greenland. We first sailed north some 30 miles until we made the Stad, a headland to our east. From there we headed straight out to sea. We have been told to sail a direct course west to Hvarf in Greenland. We are to sail north of Shetland so that we will sight land only in clear weather, south of the Faeroes, then south of Iceland so that we can see the birds and whales from there.

Passing the islands

Of the Shetlands I saw nothing, as the wind blew the sea so much as to make our passage uncomfortable. We passed the Faeroes in fine style, the wind behind us, the sun in our faces and songs on our lips.

My friends who watch where the birds fly tell me that Iceland is not far away to our north, although I cannot see it. We have yet to meet a whale, of which I am glad, as our ship, though strong, would be no match for that mighty beast of the oceans.

Heading to Greenland

We are now halfway to our destination. I long to walk on land again, as the sea here is very rough and the cold spray freezes my hands. The current pushes us south but the wind is often against us. When we get to Greenland, we will sail south and through a narrow strait and then north again towards the mountain of Hvarf. On the way we will sail into Herjolfsnes.

Journey to Mecca

At least once in their lives, Muslims try to make the hajj, or pilgrimage, to the sacred city of Mecca in Arabia. Getting there is quite straightforward today, but in the 1300s this was the journey of a lifetime.

The long way round

In 1325 Ibn Battuta set off from Tangier, Morocco, to visit the holy cities of Islam. He travelled along the North African coast to Cairo and sailed up the Nile, hoping to cross overland to the Red Sea and on to Mecca. When this failed, he returned to Cairo and trekked through Palestine and Syria before reaching Mecca in 1327.

Ibn Battuta

In 1304, Ibn Battuta was born into a wealthy family of Muslim judges, which meant that he was well educated. By the time of his death, in 1369, he had visited as many as 44 countries and travelled more than 115,000 kilometres.

Ancient wonder

Among the many amazing sights Ibn Battuta saw were the ruins of the Pharos lighthouse in Alexandria. One of the seven wonders of the ancient world, the lighthouse was built around 280 BC to guard the entrance to Alexandria.

The Pharos lighthouse, as it must once have looked.

It's Amazing!

Ibn Battuta wrote a chronicle of his journeys. Sometimes he exaggerated: he claimed he saw 12,000 bishops in a cathedral in Constantinople!

Sailing south

After his hajj, Ibn Battuta decided he would visit every Muslim country in the world. He crossed the Arabian desert to Iraq and Persia before returning to Mecca, where he studied law and religion. In 1330 he travelled down the Red Sea to the coast of East Africa.

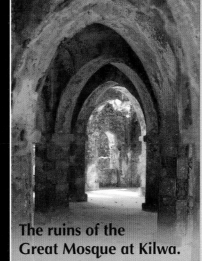
The ruins of the Great Mosque at Kilwa.

East Africa

In 1330 Ibn Battuta set out for East Africa. He visited the trading ports of Mombasa in Kenya and Kilwa in Tanzania, which he described as "one of the most beautiful and well-built of all cities". Many of the houses were built of coral and stone.

The Great Mosque in Mecca, the end point of the hajj.

Timeline

1304
Ibn Battuta born in Tangier

1325
Sets out for Cairo, and then sails up the Nile

1326
Visits Jerusalem, Damascus and Syria

1327
Reaches Mecca, travels to Persia and Iraq

1328
Returns to Mecca

1330
Travels to East Africa, sailing as far as Kilwa

To the far east

In 1331 Ibn Battuta decided to seek employment with the Sultan of Delhi, in India. Needing a guide and translator, he went to Anatolia (Turkey) to join up with traders who travelled the Silk Road into Asia.

To India and beyond

Ibn Battuta first crossed the Black Sea to Russia. He then re-crossed it in a large loop, via Constantinople, to central Asia, and on through Afghanistan to India. The sultan first employed Battuta as a judge, then offered him the post of ambassador to the Chinese emperor. Yet again, he was off on his travels. He sailed on a series of Chinese trading junks from southern India to the Chinese mainland via southeast Asia and Vietnam.

Ibn Fadlan

Ibn Battuta was not the first great Muslim traveller. In AD 921 Ibn Fadlan was sent by the Caliph of Baghdad to visit the king of the Bulgars of the Volga. He met the Rus Vikings of Russia, and was amazed by their tattoos.

It's Amazing!

Ibn Battuta was not impressed by everywhere he visited: "I did not like the land of China ... I was troubled by their worship of statues."

A break in the Maldives

On his journey from India to China, Ibn Battuta spent nine months in the Maldives in the Indian Ocean. The islands had converted from Buddhism to Islam, so he found employment as an Islamic judge. But his strict judgements were disliked among the happy-go-lucky Maldivians.

The Maldives are lush tropical islands.

Sri Lanka

Ibn Battuta was intrigued by Sri Lanka: "The entire coast of the land is littered with the trunks of the cinnamon tree." He also saw a white elephant decorated with rubies.

Cinnamon, a spice unknown in the west at this time.

The long journey home

Ibn Battuta stayed in China for a year. He then slowly made his way home, passing through the Middle East, and eventually reached Tangier in 1349. Soon he was off again, north to Muslim Spain and then south to the distant Muslim empire of Mali.

Laozi, the founder of Taoism, depicted in one of the statues Ibn Battuta objected to.

Timeline

1333
Ibn Battuta arrives in Delhi

1342
Leaves India as ambassador to China

1344
Arrives in China

1345
Travels to Damascus

1349–54
Visits Spain and Mali

1368
He dies in Tangier

Missions to the Mongols

In 1241 the Mongol armies threatened Europe. Only the death of their ruler, the Great Khan Ogedai, made their soldiers turn back. The Pope decided to make contact with the Mongols. Two Franciscan monks were sent on separate missions.

Giovanni da Pian del Carpine

The 65-year-old Giovanni and a group of monks left Lyons in France in 1245. They headed east through central Europe and Russia until they met a Mongol patrol, not far from Kiev. They reached the capital of Karakorum in June 1246. Küyük, the new Mongol leader, sent them back with the message that unless the Pope recognized his authority, "we will consider you our enemies". Giovanni had failed, but he had learned much about the Mongols.

William acted on behalf of French King Louis IX.

William of Rubruck

William of Rubruck (c.1215–95) was a Flemish Franciscan monk with a good command of foreign languages. This made him an ideal ambassador to visit the Mongols.

Gengis Khan flanked by his two sons.

The Mongol Empire

By 1206 Genghis Khan had united the various Mongol tribes. He then set out on a campaign of conquest that took the Mongol armies into the centre of Europe and south into China, Persia and the Middle East. After 1241, the empire broke up into smaller 'khanates'. By the end of the century, it had collapsed.

What Next?

The journeys of Giovanni and William opened up the road from Europe into Asia. Merchants, such as the Polo family, benefited from their journeys.

A second mission

In 1253 a second monk, William of Rubruck, left Constantinople, this time purely as a missionary. He travelled to Karakorum to meet the new khan, Möngke. William was an observant traveller, the first to realize, for example, that the Caspian Sea was landlocked. He failed to convert the Mongols, but his mission did open the way for better relations between Christian west and Mongol east.

Even today, the Mongols are skilled archers, and both men and women compete in contests.

The Mongols

The Mongols were a group of nomadic tribes from the grassy steppes north of China. Their powerful armies were highly mobile and very disciplined, which allowed them to overwhelm their enemies.

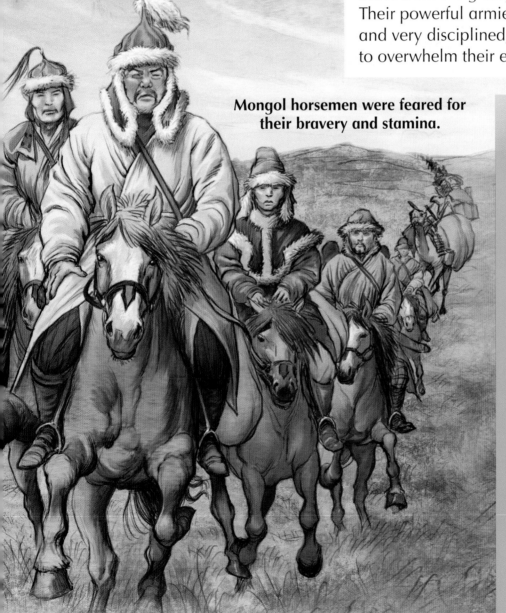

Mongol horsemen were feared for their bravery and stamina.

Timeline

1206
Mongols unite under Genghis Khan

1241
Mongol armies rampage round central Europe

1245–46
Giovanni da Pian del Carpine visits the Great Khan Küyük

1253–55
William of Rubruck visits the Great Khan Möngke

1300
Mongol power is in decline; most Mongols have converted to Islam

To China and back

At a time when people rarely ventured out of their home town or village, and very few ever left their own country to travel abroad, the exploits of the Polo family in the 1200s were indeed remarkable.

It's Amazing!
In 1298 Marco was imprisoned by the Genoese, who were at war with Venice. He told his story to fellow prisoner Rustichello, whose book, Il milione, became a bestseller.

Timeline

1254
Marco Polo born in Venice

1259–69
Niccolo and Mafeo Polo make their first journey to China

1271–75
The Polos return to China with Marco

1295
The Polos arrive back in Venice

1298–99
Imprisoned by the Genoese, Marco Polo dictates *Il milione*, an account of his travels

1324
Marco Polo dies in Venice

Trading places

Niccolo and Mafeo Polo were merchants from Venice in Italy, who were keen to trade with the wealthy Mongol Empire of China. In 1259 they journeyed through Russia and central Asia as far as Khanbaliq (Beijing), the capital of the Mongol Empire. Here they met the emperor, Kublai Khan. The two brothers returned to Venice in 1269.

The court of Kublai Khan

The Polos returned to China in 1271, this time with Niccolo's son, the 17-year-old Marco. They arrived at the summer palace of Kublai Khan (left) in Shang-du in May 1275.

Marco Polo

Marco Polo (1254–1324) was taken to China as a teenager. He worked for the Mongol emperor Kublai Khan for 20 years, becoming one of his most trusted servants. Polo spent much of this time travelling around China and Asia and learning about the region. In the 1290s, Marco returned to Venice with his father and uncle.

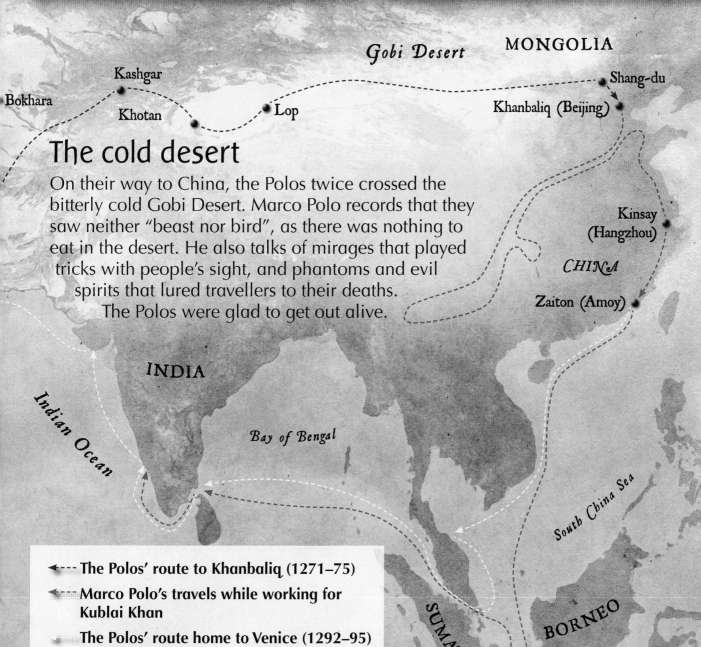

MONGOLIA

Gobi Desert

Kashgar

Shang-du

Bokhara

Khanbaliq (Beijing)

Khotan

Lop

The cold desert

On their way to China, the Polos twice crossed the bitterly cold Gobi Desert. Marco Polo records that they saw neither "beast nor bird", as there was nothing to eat in the desert. He also talks of mirages that played tricks with people's sight, and phantoms and evil spirits that lured travellers to their deaths. The Polos were glad to get out alive.

Kinsay (Hangzhou)

CHINA

Zaiton (Amoy)

INDIA

Indian Ocean

Bay of Bengal

South China Sea

◄---- The Polos' route to Khanbaliq (1271–75)

◄---- Marco Polo's travels while working for Kublai Khan

◄--- The Polos' route home to Venice (1292–95)

SUMATRA

BORNEO

JAVA

The seven voyages of Zheng He

In 1405, Emperor Yongle ruled over the Ming Empire in China. To show his neighbours just how powerful his empire was, Yongle sent a naval expedition to sail round the region, led by the court official Zheng He.

The imperial fleet

Zheng He commanded an impressive fleet of over 300 sea-going junks. The largest was 140 metres long and had nine masts. More than 28,000 sailors were required to sail this vast fleet, which was designed to impress, not to conquer territory. When each region's ruler saw at first hand the power of the Ming Empire, he would happily acknowledge that Yongle was the most powerful emperor of all.

Timeline

1371
Zheng He born in Yunnan province

1402
Yongle becomes the third Ming emperor

1405–07
Zheng He's first voyage, to southeast Asia and India

1407–22
Zheng He makes five more voyages

1426
New emperor Xuande withdraws support from Zheng He

1433
Zheng He dies at sea during his seventh voyage

Emperor Yongle, Zhu Yuanzhang's son and the third emperor of the Ming Dynasty.

The Ming Dynasty

In 1356 the Chinese, led by a peasant and former Buddhist monk, Zhu Yuanzhang, rose up against their Mongol overlords. Zhu seized Beijing, the Mongol capital, in 1368. He declared himself Emperor Hongwu, first of the new Ming Dynasty. The Ming brought great wealth to China until they were overthrown by the Manchus in 1644.

China from China

In the mid-1300s Chinese potters began to make pure, white porcelain decorated with bright cobalt blue. Zheng He gave porcelain to the kings he met on his travels. In return he was given animals such as zebras and giraffes, which he took back to the zoo in Beijing.

A late Ming dynasty blue-and-white porcelain plate dating from the 16th century.

The Forbidden City in Beijing, built after Emperor Yongle made Beijing the Chinese capital in 1420.

The voyages

Zheng He made seven voyages between 1405 and 1433. His first three voyages took him round southeast Asia and on to India and Sri Lanka. On later voyages he reached as far west as Arabia and the east African coast. Everywhere he went, he handed out Chinese silks, porcelain and other fine goods. In total, Zheng He visited more than 30 kingdoms. He died on a voyage round the Indian Ocean.

It's Amazing!

The records of Zheng He's last two voyages were destroyed. He may have visited the west coast of America and New Zealand.

Pointing the way

Around AD 1100, the Chinese discovered that a magnetized needle always points in the same direction. They used this discovery to make a compass to help sailors find their way on their voyages.

A Chinese box compass.

EUROPE LOOKS EAST

Europeans have long been fascinated by Asia. The usual route between the continents was by land along the Silk Road. However, in the 1400s the Portuguese began to search for a sea route round Africa that would take them to India and China. Missionaries and adventurers followed in their wake. During the 1600s the Russians began to explore the vast empire they had created in Siberia. In recent times, Europeans have explored the most remote regions of Asia.

Prince Henry the Navigator

Henry the Navigator was a 15th-century Portuguese prince. Although he did no exploring himself, it could be said that he did more for exploration than anyone before or since.

An interest in Africa

In 1415 the Portuguese seized the city of Ceuta in Morocco from its Muslim rulers. Among the victorious army was Prince Henrique (Henry), son of King João I. The campaign inspired Henry to learn more about Africa. With his father's support, he set up a school of navigation at Sagres in southwest Portugal. From here, fleets of ships set out to explore the west African coastline.

Prince Henry

Prince Henry (1394–1460) used his personal wealth to sponsor voyages. He encouraged Portuguese sailors to investigate the lands and oceans to their south.

The navigation school

Founded in 1418, the navigation school at Sagres taught map-making, geography and astronomy, all essential tools for any explorer. Armed with these skills, Portuguese captains and pilots were able to map new lands so that future expeditions could benefit from their experience.

A Portuguese map from 1485 showing the west coasts of Europe and Africa.

New route to Asia

In 1453 the Portuguese voyages assumed a new urgency. The Muslim Ottoman Turks had taken the city of Constantinople and totally blocked the Silk Road from Europe to Asia. The Portuguese needed to discover a sea route round Africa that would take them to the wealth of India and China.

A drawing of a caravel from the 15th century.

The caravel

The Portuguese developed a new type of ship known as the caravel. Narrower than its predecessors, the caravel was easy to manoeuvre and better able to withstand storms. It had a hold in which to store the supplies necessary for a long voyage.

What Next?

The navigational skills and better ships developed by the Portuguese ultimately allowed European nations to dominate the world's seas, and the lands around them.

A contemporary picture of the Portuguese capital, Lisbon.

Timeline

1415
Portuguese capture Ceuta in Africa

1418
Prince Henry founds navigation school

1427
Portuguese sailors begin exploring the west African coast

1444
Portuguese reach the Senegal River

1471
Trading post at Elmina in Ghana is established

1472
Lopo Gonçalves is first European to cross the equator

Edging down the coast

By 1480 the Portuguese had crossed the equator and begun to map the coastline of southern Africa. They still did not know if they would find a sea route to India and the east, because the African coast seemed to go on forever.

Diogo Cão

The voyages of Portuguese explorer Diogo Cão (c.1450–86) did much to open up the sea route to India. His mapping of the River Congo helped many future navigators in the region.

Cão's first voyage

In 1482 Diogo Cão set off from the capital, Lisbon. He sailed down the North African coast and stopped for supplies at the fort of Elmina in Ghana. He then turned south. When Cão reached the mouth of the River Congo, he erected a stone padrão, or pillar, on its southern bank. He sailed upstream hoping it would lead him round Africa, before turning back.

The fort of Elmina in Ghana was used by the Portuguese for trade, including the slave trade.

Timeline

1482
Diogo Cão sails south to the River Congo via Elmina in Ghana. Sails as far as Cape Santa Maria in Angola before returning home

1484
Arrives back in Lisbon and is knighted by the king for his efforts

1484–85
Cão returns to the River Congo and sails upstream before rapids force him to turn back

1486
Sails south to Cape Cross where he dies

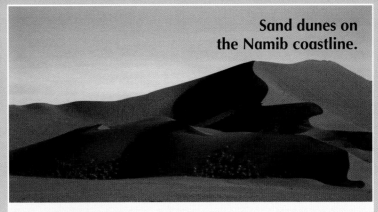

Sand dunes on the Namib coastline.

Namibia

Diogo Cão sailed down the coast of Namibia but found it to be a hot desert with no natural harbours. He died somewhere off Cape Cross, a few kilometres away from Walvis Bay, one of the finest natural harbours on the entire coast.

Pushing south

In 1482, Cão sailed south to Cape Santa Maria in Angola, where he erected a padrão before returning to Lisbon. In 1484 he set off again, this time sailing right up the Congo before rapids closed his route. He then headed even further south, erecting a padrão at Cape Cross in Namibia. At this point, his life ended, either shipwrecked on Cape Cross or lost at sea.

It's Amazing!

King João II sponsored Cão's second voyage in 1484 rather than support a voyage across the Atlantic proposed by Christopher Columbus.

The padrão

King João gave Diogo Cão 1.5-m-high limestone padrãos, or pillars, each topped with a cross and inscribed with the names of the king and the expedition commander. Cão placed the pillars in significant places to guide future explorers.

A limestone padrão with the Portuguese royal coat of arms carved on it.

Reaching the Indian Ocean

By 1487 the Portuguese had mapped most of the west African coastline, but there appeared to be no route round it to India. One man, Bartolomeu Dias, proved this to be wrong.

The end of Africa

In 1487 Dias sailed out of Lisbon with two caravels and one supply ship. By the end of the year he had made it south of Cape Cross. After passing the Orange River, a huge storm blew up that forced him in a southerly direction for 13 days. When it calmed, he headed east, expecting land. Instead, he found more sea.

The Cape of Good Hope on the southwest tip of Africa.

Cape of Good Hope

As Dias sailed west on his voyage home, he caught his first sight of the Cape of Good Hope. The name was suggested by Dias, although some historians credit King João with naming it.

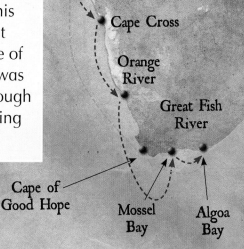

EUROPE

Lisbon

- - - → outbound journey
← - - - inbound journey

Cape Verde

Elmina

AFRICA

Atlantic Ocean

River Congo

Cape Cross

Orange River

Great Fish River

Cape of Good Hope

Mossel Bay

Algoa Bay

Bartolomeu Dias

Bartolomeu Dias (c.1450–1500) added some 2016 kilometres to the length of African coastline known to Europeans. After his own successful voyage, he accompanied Vasco da Gama on the first leg of his voyage to India in 1497. He was also one of the commanders in Pedro Cabral's fleet that discovered Brazil in 1500. He died later in the same expedition.

It's Amazing!

Dias was the first navigator to take a spare ship filled with supplies. He left it off the west African coast, but returned to find that the provisions had been looted.

Into the Indian Ocean

Dias turned north, landing at present-day Mossel Bay, 320 kilometres east of the Cape of Good Hope. He then sailed further east to Algoa Bay and then on to a river he named the Rio de Infante, probably the one known today as the Great Fish River, where he erected a padrão. By now Dias was in the Indian Ocean, having rounded the southern tip of Africa. When his crew forced him to return, he sailed back west along the coast, sighting the Cape of Good Hope before he turned north to Elmina.

Indian Ocean

Timeline

1487
Dias sets sail from Lisbon with a fleet of three ships

1488
Dias is blown south by a storm and sails past the Cape of Good Hope into the Southern Ocean

1488
Enters Indian Ocean

1497
Sails with Vasco da Gama

1500
Dias sails with Cabral, discovering Brazil, then dies in a storm

The route to India

Now that Bartolomeu Dias had discovered a route round Africa into the Indian Ocean, the sea route was open to India and the east. The man to open that route up was Vasco da Gama.

Around the Cape

Da Gama set sail from Lisbon in July 1497. He stopped in the Cape Verde Islands for a week in July and then headed south into the Atlantic, away from the unpredictable winds and tides along the African coast. After 96 days he made landfall in St Helena Bay on the west coast of South Africa. From there he edged round the Cape of Good Hope into the Indian Ocean and up the east coast of Africa to Mombasa and Malindi in Kenya.

Vasco da Gama

Vasco da Gama (c.1460–1524) was a ruthless Portuguese sailor whose voyage to India in 1497 opened up a new sea route to the east. Honoured by King Manuel I as Admiral of India, da Gama returned in 1502 to win control over the spice trade.

A Portuguese map of India from the 16th century.

Da Gama made a bad impression when he met the ruler of Calicut.

In Calicut

Once in India, da Gama met the Hindu ruler of Calicut, but the gifts he offered him were poor quality. The Muslims who controlled the spice trade in the region feared Portuguese intentions, and tried to get the local Hindus to destroy their fleet. Da Gama was lucky to get away.

Navigation tools

Early navigators used an astrolabe or a quadrant to work out latitude – how far north or south the ship was. The astrolabe measured the height of the Sun, the quadrant the height of a star. It was not possible to measure longitude – how far east or west – accurately until the mid-18th century.

An early astrolabe, used to calculate latitude.

To India and back

Da Gama headed northeast from Malindi across the Indian Ocean. The favourable winds took him straight to Calicut in southern India, where he made landfall in May 1498. His mission accomplished, he set off home in August. His return was much harder because of unfavourable winds in the Indian Ocean, and he did not reach Lisbon until September 1499.

Timeline

1497
Da Gama leaves Lisbon with four ships

1498
Sails up the east African coast and across the Indian Ocean to Calicut

1499
Reaches Lisbon with one ship and a quarter of his crew still alive

1502–03
Returns to India and ruthlessly enforces Portuguese control over the spice trade

1524
Da Gama dies in India

It's Amazing!
Da Gama's expedition led to the establishment of colonies in India, which remained in Portuguese hands until 1961.

A Portuguese sailor

Prince Henry the Navigator sponsored many voyages to explore the coastline of Africa. One set sail in 1456 under the Venetian Alvise da Cadamosto (1432–c.1480). They sailed up the River Gambia, noting the mighty baobab tree and the hippo. Here we imagine the diary of a member of the crew.

The voyage south

I sail on board a caravel under the captaincy of Alvise da Cadamosto, a man from the port of Venice although I myself come from our capital, Lisbon. We sail south to explore the coastline of Africa so that our knowledge of it might lead to good trade, or perhaps to convert its heathen people to the way of our Lord.

Cape Verde Islands

After we left the islands of the Canaries, we sailed past Cape Branco and into the open sea. I have not sailed without sight of land before and feared for my safety. God be praised, no harm came to us, and we made our passage safely.

A mighty storm raged for three days and blew us off our course. When the storm calmed, we saw two islands that we later found were empty of people. We have named these islands Boavista and Santiago and claimed them for our king.

Up the River Gambia

We left these islands some days past and headed east to Africa. We sailed up a great river, about which I have much to tell. Enormous trees that measure seventeen feet around their trunks line the river banks. There are many strange beasts, such as the elephant and an animal that some call a water horse, but looks more like a giant pig to me. It is over ten feet long and has very short legs and cloven hooves. On its head there are two tusks, each almost as long as a forearm. Other creatures watch us from the bank. Some look like small hairy people and chatter to each other.

The local people are called Mandingos, and treat us with respect but are afraid of our guns. They took our captain to meet their king, Batti Mansa. It is said that they traded gold and wild animals. They fed our captain the meat of an elephant, which he heartily disliked.

Travellers and missionaries

The voyages of early navigators opened up the coastline of Asia to European traders. But it was not until the mid-1500s that European missionaries began to explore inland.

Missionary zeal

The Jesuit order was determined to convert Asia to Christianity. Spanish priest Francis Xavier was the first to go. He was followed by the Portuguese Bento de Goes (1562–1607), who from 1602–07 travelled through central Asia into China in search of a lost Christian community.

Saint Francis Xavier

The son of a Basque nobleman, Francis Xavier (1506–52) was a founder member of the Jesuits. He spent several years in India and Sri Lanka before sailing for Japan, where he arrived in 1549. He was made a saint after baptizing the most people since St Paul.

A 17th-century painting of St Francis Xavier by Andre Reinoso.

The body of Saint Francis Xavier on display in Goa, India.

The Jesuits

The Society of Jesus, also called the Jesuits, is a Roman Catholic religious order. It was founded by Ignatius Loyola and six other trainee priests in 1534, originally to convert Muslims to Christianity. It soon widened its activities to cover India and China.

The seal of the Society of Jesus.

The forbidden city

Two Jesuits, German John Grueber (1623–80) and Belgian Albert d'Orville (1621–62) set out in 1661 to find a land route between China and India to avoid Dutch raiders on the China Sea. They crossed the Himalayas, becoming the first Europeans to visit the sacred city of Lhasa in Tibet.

It's Amazing!

St Francis Xavier died off the coast of China. His body was brought to Goa, but his right forearm, which he used to baptize converts, was removed and taken to Rome.

A Tibetan yak, well adapted for life on the 'roof of the world'.

A strange continent

European knowledge of Asia was still extremely vague in the 1600s. Grueber and d'Orville were amazed when, travelling into Tibet, they exchanged their horses for strange beasts of burden called yaks.

Timeline

1541–52
Francis Xavier visits India, Sri Lanka, China and Japan to convert people to Christianity

1602–07
Bento de Goes seeks lost Christian community said to exist between China and India

1624–26
Antonio de Andrade becomes first European to cross the Himalayas

1661
Grueber and d'Orville travel from China through Tibet to India

Into Siberia

During the 1600s, the Russian Empire expanded eastwards across Siberia to the Pacific Ocean. The Russian tzar Peter the Great knew little about his new realm, and decided to find out more.

Heading east

In 1724 Peter appointed Vitus Bering to lead an expedition of discovery to Siberia. His task was to travel overland to the Pacific coastline of the Kamchatka peninsula in eastern Siberia. He was then to sail north to discover whether Siberia and Asia were connected to North America.

Asia

North America

The Bering Strait, which separates Asia from North America, as seen from space.

Vitus Bering

Vitus Bering (1681–1741) was born in Denmark, and became one of the hundreds of western Europeans recruited by Peter the Great to modernize his backward country. Bering was a superb organizer, and twice arranged large-scale expeditions to one of the most remote places on the Earth.

Peter the Great

Peter the Great (reigned 1682–1725) turned his country into a powerful nation. In 1697 he travelled to Europe to learn about shipbuilding and returned home to build a great navy. He moved the national capital to a new city, St Petersburg, and defeated Sweden to gain an outlet to the Baltic.

What Next?
Russian settlers established the first settlement in Alaska in 1784. Russia eventually sold Alaska to the USA in 1867 for $7.2 million.

The *St Peter* and *St Paul*.

Bering's ships

Bering was a skilled shipbuilder. He twice built small ships to sail from Okhotsk to Kamchatka. He then built three sea-going ships to explore the strait between Asia and North America: the *St Gabriel* on his first expedition, the *St Peter* and *St Paul* on his second.

Timeline

1724
Vitus Bering commands expedition to Siberia

1727
Bering and his team arrive in Okhotsk on the Siberian coast

1728
After crossing Kamchatka, he sets sail north, turning south a month later

1729
Bering retraces his steps across Siberia

1730
Back in St Petersburg Bering fails to convince everyone that he completed the task

Qualified success

In 1728, Bering sailed northwards up the Pacific coast of Siberia into the strait that separates Siberia from Alaska and now bears his name. Fog prevented him from seeing land but Bering was convinced that the two continents were not joined. Back in St Petersburg, however, the authorities were not convinced, and ordered Bering to go back.

Mapping the North

In 1733 Vitus Bering set off once more for Siberia, this time in charge of one of the most ambitious explorations ever organized. The Great Northern Expedition aimed to map the entire coastline of Siberia, as well as many of the region's great rivers.

The death of Bering

It took Bering eight years to travel beyond Siberia. He finally set sail from Kamchatka to Alaska in June 1741. He sailed to the south Alaskan coast but, sick and short of food, he was forced to make his way back via the Aleutian Islands. In November 1741 Bering and his crew were shipwrecked on the island that is now named after him. Bering died, but his crew survived and sailed home the following year.

Alexei Chirikov

Captain Alexei Chirikov (1703–48) was Bering's second-in-command. Chirikov lost contact with Bering off Alaska but he managed to get his ship and crew back to Siberia, although many lost their lives to scurvy and hostile Inuits in Alaska.

Vitus Bering died while he and his crew were iced in on the island that is now named after him.

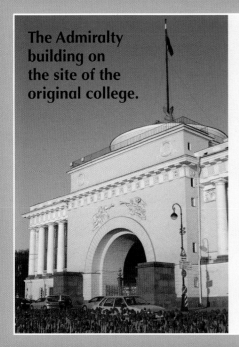

The Admiralty building on the site of the original college.

Imperial Admiralty College

The Great Northern Expedition was organized by the Imperial Admiralty College in St Petersburg. Vitus Bering was given the task of travelling to the Pacific, while groups of naval officers divided the exploration of the north coast of Siberia and its rivers between them.

Exploring Siberia

The rest of the expedition had much more success. The great Ob, Yenisei and Lena rivers that flow north into the Arctic Ocean were all explored. So was the Arctic coast from Archangel in the west to the Kolyma River in the far east of Siberia. The teams had plenty of manpower, but there was little back-up and fewer supplies. They were often not heard of for years at a time.

Timeline

1733
The Great Northern Expedition sets off for Siberia

1735–41
Teams explore the Arctic coastline and Siberian rivers

1741
Bering and Chirikov set sail from Petropavlovsk in Kamchatka to southern Alaskan coast; Bering dies on the return journey

1742
Semion Chelyuskin discovers Cape Chelyuskin, the northernmost point of Siberia

Wolf carcasses hang up waiting to be skinned.

Fur trappers

The expedition into Siberia opened the way for fur trappers and traders to exploit the animal wealth of the region. Mink, sable, bear and other wild animals were all trapped for their valuable furs and skins.

It's Amazing!
After Bering died, his crew built a small boat out of the wreckage of their ship, the St Peter, and used it to sail to safety.

Along the Silk Road

Although Europeans had learned much about Asia by the 19th century, the center of the continent between the Russian, Chinese, and British Indian empires was largely unknown. Tibet was still forbidden territory, while the old Silk Road had largely been forgotten.

The Cave of the Thousand Buddhas, visited by Aurel Stein in 1907.

Crossing the deserts

In 1890, the Swedish explorer Sven Hedin set out on the first of his four epic expeditions. During 45 years, he mapped large parts of central Asia, exploring the Silk Road and crossing the vast Taklimakan and Gobi deserts of western China and Mongolia. His only failure occurred in 1901, when he tried but failed to enter the forbidden holy city of Lhasa in Tibet.

Sven Hedin, centre, holding one of his maps.

Sven Hedin

The Swedish explorer Sven Hedin (1865–1952) was a skilled linguist. He worked as a diplomat and interpreter for the Swedish government, which sponsored two of his expeditions. On his final expedition, from 1933–35, he completed a detailed map of the old Silk Road for the Chinese government.

Timeline

1890
Sven Hedin begins first of four expeditions

1899–1902
Hedin discovers the ancient city of Lou-lan in the Taklimakan Desert

1900–02
Aurel Stein explores the Taklimakan Desert

1906–08
Hedin finds the source of the Indus and Brahmaputra rivers

1907
Aurel Stein discovers the *Diamond Sutra*

1933–35
Hedin maps Silk Road

The Tilla-Kari Medrassa in Samarkand, visited by Stein in 1914.

The intrepid archaeologist

Sir Marc Aurel Stein (1862–1943) was a Hungarian archaeologist who became a British citizen. He led four major expeditions in central Asia after 1900, travelling more than 40,000 kilometres and collecting ancient artefacts and manuscripts.

Collector or thief?

Inspired by Hedin, the British archeologist Sir Marc Aurel Stein explored the Chinese end of the Silk Road, looking for ancient documents to bring back to Great Britain for research. Although Stein's discoveries were really important, many people criticized his methods: the Chinese called him a "foreign devil," robbing them of their archeological heritage.

The *Diamond Sutra*

In 1907 Aurel Stein discovered 40,000 scrolls in the Cave of the Thousand Buddhas at Dunhuang in western China. Among them was the *Diamond Sutra*, the world's oldest known printed book, dating from AD 868.

The *Diamond Sutra*, a short collection of Buddhist teachings.

Into Arabia

Among the parts of Asia least known to Europeans were the deserts of Syria and Arabia, and the two Muslim holy cities of Mecca and Medina, both closed to non-Muslims. During the 19th century, a number of Europeans visited this remote area and were amazed at what they found.

It's Amazing!

Petra is entered through a narrow gap in the rocks only three to four metres wide. A monastery, church, tombs and other buildings have been carved out of the solid red rock.

Forgotten city

Johann Ludwig Burckhardt arrived in Syria under the assumed name of Sheikh Ibrahim ibn Abdullah. In 1812, he headed south towards Egypt and visited Petra, a city carved into solid rock from the 2nd century BC. He was the first Westerner in modern times to visit the forgotten city, which only became fully accessible to foreigners in the 1920s.

Petra, described by poet J W Burgon as the "rose-red city half as old as time".

Burckhardt, disguised as an Arab sheikh.

Johann Ludwig Burckhardt

Johann Ludwig Burckhardt (1784–1817) was born in Lausanne, Switzerland. When he moved to London in 1806, Burckhardt became intrigued by the idea of visiting foreign lands. He travelled first to Syria and then to Egypt and Arabia before dying of dysentery in Cairo.

The holy cities

After some time in Egypt, a disguised Burckhardt crossed the Red Sea and visited Mecca and Medina. Explorers Richard Burton and Charles Doughty followed in his path, but Doughty was much more interested in the Bedouin who lived in the surrounding desert.

T E Lawrence, a great admirer of Doughty's book.

Arabia Deserta

The English explorer Charles Doughty lived for two years with the Bedouin of the Syrian and Arabian deserts. In 1888 he published his journal, *Travels in Arabia Deserta*. The book was little known until it was championed in the 1920s by famed scholar T E Lawrence.

Desert dwellers

The Bedouin are semi-nomadic tribesmen who live in the deserts of Syria and Arabia. They travel with their flocks in search of water and the occasional pasture. They live in tents and are immensely skilled at coping with the intense heat and lack of water.

A Bedouin encampment in the desert.

Timeline

1812
Johann Ludwig Burckhardt is the first Westerner to visit Petra

1814–15
Burckhardt visits Mecca and Medina

1815–16
Burckhardt visits the ancient monasteries on the Sinai Peninsula

1853
Richard Burton visits the holy cities dressed as an Afghan doctor

1876–78
Charles Doughty lives with the Bedouin of Arabia

The Empty Quarter

In the last century, most of the world was explored, its peoples visited and its cultures described. Modern travellers have therefore sought out the most inaccessible areas, and the most distant and self-sufficient peoples.

Across the desert

The desert of southeast Saudi Arabia is known as the Rub' al Khali, the Empty Quarter, as it has no roads and few people or animals. Bertram Thomas crossed the Rub' al Khali in 1930–31, the first European to do so. His book *Arabia Felix* (1932) describes the desert's people and their culture.

Bertram Thomas

Bertram Thomas (1892–1950) was a British civil servant who, in 1925, became finance minister to the Sultan of Oman. As part of his duties, he made several expeditions into the desert.

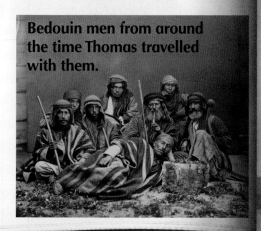

Bedouin men from around the time Thomas travelled with them.

Timeline

1925–32
Bertram Thomas is finance minister to the Sultan of Oman

1930–31
Thomas crosses the Empty Quarter

1945–49
Wilfred Thesiger travels around the Empty Quarter, maps the Liwa oasis and the Umm As-Sammim quicksands

1951–58
Thesiger lives with the Marsh Arabs of Iraq

Wilfred Thesiger travelling with the Bedouin in the Arabian Desert.

Wilfred Thesiger

Wilfred Thesiger (1910–2003) was born the son of a British diplomat in Addis Ababa, capital of Ethiopia. He travelled all his life and, in the 1930s, he was the first European to visit parts of northern Ethiopia. Later, he travelled extensively around Saudi Arabia, Iraq and Kenya.

Thesiger took thousands of photographs using a Leica 2 similar to this one.

The wanderer

By his own words, Wilfred Thesiger had a "strange compulsion" to wander the deserts of the world, living as the people of the area lived. His travels took him to Africa, the mountains of central Asia and the deserts of Arabia. Between 1945–49, Thesiger explored the entire Empty Quarter. He particularly admired the Bedouin way of life.

Reed boats such as this are the Marsh Arabs' main form of transport.

The Marsh Arabs

The Marsh Arabs are the inhabitants of the marsh islands in southern Iraq. They live by raising water buffalo, growing crops and weaving reeds. The area has always been isolated from the rest of Iraq and provided a shelter for escaped slaves.

What Next?

In the 1990s, Saddam Hussein, then dictator of Iraq, tried to drain the marshes and expel the Marsh Arabs. Today, only a few thousand of the original half a million inhabitants remain.

Intrepid women

Almost all explorers have been men, as women have traditionally lacked the independence to travel for themselves. However, during the early 20th century, two women became renowned explorers.

Caspian Sea

Elburz Mountains

◎ Alamut

◎ Tehran

◎ Mosul   P E R S I A

◎ Kirkuk

River Euphrates   I R A Q   *River Tigris*

Palmyra ◎

◎ Damascus   Ar Ramadi   ◎ Baghdad.

◎ Amman

Mediterranean sea

P A L E S T I N E   T R A N S - J O R D A N   ◎ An Najaf

◎ Al Jawf

S E B E L   S H A M M A R   Kuwait ◎

◎ Hail   *Persian Gulf*

- ╌╌► **Gertrude Bell's journey to central Arabia 1913–14**
- ◎ **Places visited by Freya Stark while based in Baghdad 1928–32**
- ◎ **Towns on Gertrude Bell's route**

Setting the border

In 1905 British archaeologist Gertrude Bell first explored the Syrian desert. She almost lost her life on another expedition into central Arabia in 1913. From 1916 till her death in 1926, Bell worked for the British government helping to set up the new country of Iraq.

Red sea

N
W   E
S

The high Elburz Mountains in Iran, which Stark crossed to reach the Hashshashin castle at Alamut.

The travel writer

Freya Stark (1893–1993) developed a taste for travelling alone in the roughest, most remote areas. She learned Arabic and in 1927 set out for Arabia, travelling with the Bedouin. She wrote books about her many journeys, and said that "to awaken quite alone in a strange town is one of the most pleasant sensations in the world".

A lone traveller

Freya Stark was fascinated by the Hashshashin, a feared medieval Muslim sect. They carried out many daring missions to murder their enemies, and gave us our word *assassin*, meaning killer. Stark visited their castle at Alamut in northern Persia (now Iran) in 1930, and returned a year later to map the area. Stark travelled around the Arabian desert in the years that followed and continued to explore the Middle East until the 1950s.

Gertrude Bell

Gertrude Bell (1868–1926) first visited Persia (Iran) in 1892, when her uncle served in the British embassy. She fell in love with the culture, and devoted most of her adult life to studying the Middle East.

Timeline

1899
Gertrude Bell tours Palestine and Syria

1909
Bell first visits Mesopotamia (now Iraq)

1913–14
Bell travels from Syria to Iraq and into Arabia

1916–26
Bell helps set up the new state of Iraq

1927–28
Freya Stark travels through Arabia

1928–32
Based in Baghdad, Stark travels extensively round the Middle East

1933–39
Stark travels alone in the Arabian desert

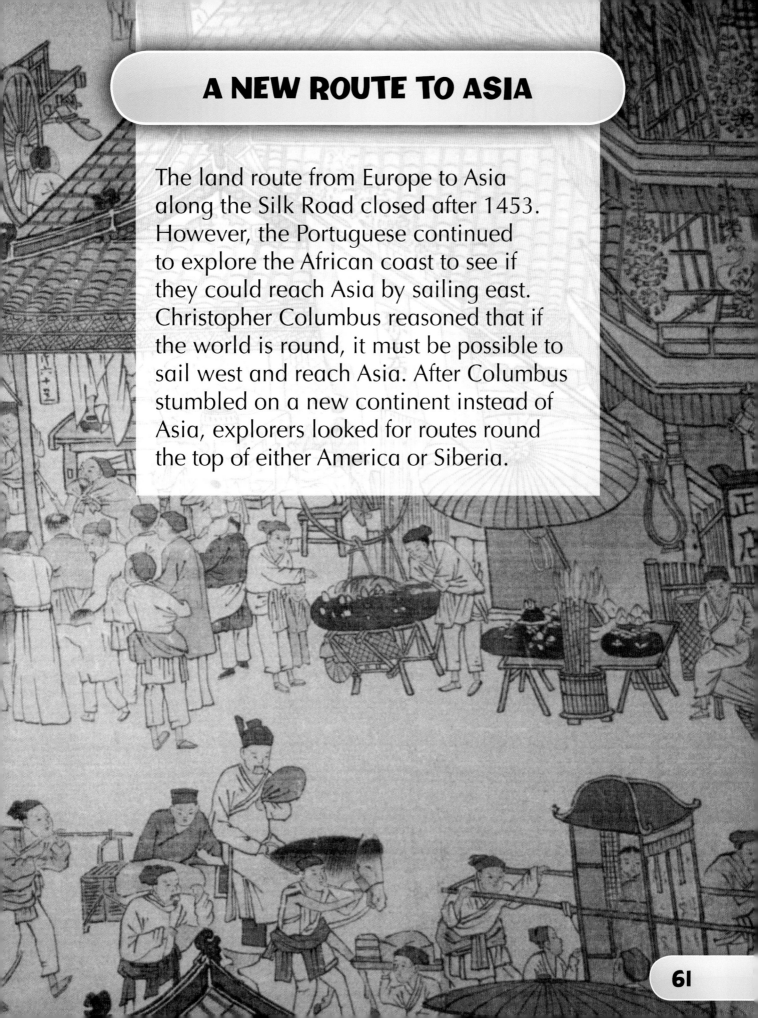

A NEW ROUTE TO ASIA

The land route from Europe to Asia along the Silk Road closed after 1453. However, the Portuguese continued to explore the African coast to see if they could reach Asia by sailing east. Christopher Columbus reasoned that if the world is round, it must be possible to sail west and reach Asia. After Columbus stumbled on a new continent instead of Asia, explorers looked for routes round the top of either America or Siberia.

Columbus's first voyage

Italian Christopher Columbus dreamed of sailing west from Europe to reach Cipangu (Japan). In 1491 King Ferdinand and Queen Isabella of Spain agreed to fund his voyage.

The fleet

On 3 August 1492 Columbus set sail from the Spanish port of Palos with three ships: the three-masted cargo ship, *Santa Maria*, the three-masted caravel, the *Niña*, and the four-masted caravel, the *Pinta*. After a stop in the Canary Islands, the fleet set off again on 6 September.

It's a Mystery!

Columbus landed on an island he named San Salvador. Historians have suggested nine possible places in the Bahamas, but nobody really knows where Columbus landed.

Columbus's fleet, the *Niña*, the *Santa Maria* (centre) and the *Pinta*.

Columbus

Christopher Columbus (c.1451–1506) was born in the Italian port of Genoa. Remarkably little is know about his early life. In 1476 he moved to Lisbon and married a Portuguese noblewoman. He died in Spain in 1506.

The pineapple, one of many new foods eaten by Columbus.

New discoveries

Columbus did not find gold or rich trading cities in the lands he thought were Asia, but he and his crew did eat new foods such as pineapples, potatoes and sweetcorn. He also observed the Arawaks smoking tobacco leaves in a pipe.

A new world?

In the night of 12 October, the lookout on the *Pinta* saw land. Columbus and crew landed on the island they named San Salvador and claimed it for Spain. Columbus was convinced he had landed off the west coast of India so he named these islands the West Indies. He would never know he had discovered a continent that was previously unknown to Europeans.

The Arawaks

On San Salvador, Columbus traded glass beads with the native Arawaks in return for parrots and "a kind of dry leaf", tobacco. The Arawaks told him of a king to the south who had much gold, and Columbus set off to find him. The Arawaks soon died of diseases brought by Europeans, for which they had no immunity.

Timeline

3 August 1492
Columbus sets sail with three ships and a crew of 85 from Palos in Spain

12 October
Land is sighted two hours after midnight

28 October
Columbus reaches Cuba and sails along the coast before sailing to Hispaniola

25 December
While exploring the Hispaniola coastline, the *Santa Maria* runs aground and is abandoned

16 January 1493
After establishing a colony in what is now Haiti, Columbus returns to Spain

Arawak musicians danced as they played.

On board with Columbus

Rodrigo de Triana sailed with Columbus on board the Pinta, a four-masted caravel. He was the first European since the Vikings to see the coast of the Americas, but his achievement went unrewarded. Columbus wrote his version of events in a diary. Here is what Rodrigo thought.

(Rodrigo de Triana is real. His diary is made up.)

Across the ocean

3 AUGUST 1492 We left sight of Palos this day, and with it my beloved homeland of Spain. We are heading west. I trust my captain, Don Martin Alonso Pinzón, and the commander of our fleet, Don Christopher Columbus, but I fear what lies ahead, for it is unknown. Don Christopher hopes to sail to Asia, and we can only pray that we arrive there safely.

13 AUGUST We sight the islands of the Canaries, and I am relieved to see land again. We will wait here while the rudder of our ship is repaired and the Niña is given a new rig to make her safe to cross this great ocean.

16 SEPTEMBER The sea around is suddenly full with tufts of bright green grass. There is so much seaweed that the ocean looks like a vast meadow. I think we must be near land, but I see none ahead. The wind is very light and blows, when it does, from all directions.

A false alarm

26 SEPTEMBER Yesterday was a day I wish to forget. Just after high noon, I thought I saw land out to the west, and shouted the good news to my captain. But I was wrong, and I have been punished for my mistake.

7 OCTOBER Flocks of birds fly past us overhead in the direction of the south west. Don Christopher has given orders that we change direction to follow them.

Land ahoy!

12 OCTOBER Last night Don Christopher thought he saw a light to the west that he said was "like a little wax candle bobbing up and down". Then, at two hours past midnight this morning, I spied land. This morning, Don Christopher and some crew, including me, landed on this isle. We christened it San Salvador.

Gulf of Mexico

San Salvador

Juana

Atlantic Ocean

Hispanola

N

W   E

Santiago

S

San Juan Bautista

Caribbean Sea

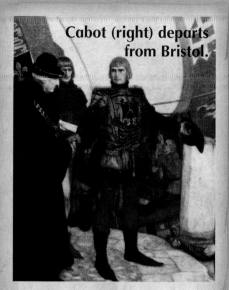

Cabot (right) departs from Bristol.

John Cabot

John Cabot, or Giovanni Caboto, was born in Italy in about 1450 and died around 1498. He settled in Bristol, England, where he hoped to find sponsors for his voyage. His son, Sebastian (1476–1557), was also a noted explorer.

The new-found land

When Columbus returned to Europe in 1493 with news of his 'discovery' of a new route to Asia, other navigators quickly followed him. Italian sailor John Cabot decided to sail a shorter route.

Sailing north

Spices arriving in England via the Middle East were very expensive, so merchants were interested in finding a shorter route to the east. Cabot knew that the shortest route to Asia would be to sail across the Atlantic Ocean at as northerly a latitude as possible. He presented his proposals to Henry VII of England.

The Newfoundland coast, where Cabot probably landed in 1497.

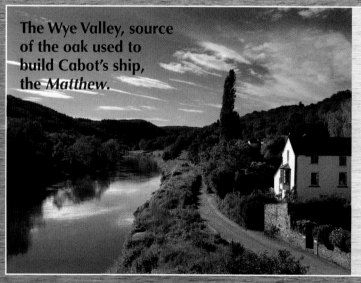

The Wye Valley, source of the oak used to build Cabot's ship, the *Matthew*.

A wealthy sponsor

Richard Amerike was a wealthy Welsh merchant who became Sheriff of Bristol in 1503. Amerike sponsored Cabot's two voyages, and some historians believe that Cabot named the new lands he found after his generous sponsor.

Canadian landfall

Henry VII agreed to support the voyage, so in 1497 Cabot set off from Bristol on board the *Matthew*. He landed in North America, probably on the island of Newfoundland or possibly further south at Nova Scotia, both in modern-day Canada. In 1498 Cabot set off again, this time with five ships, but was never heard of again.

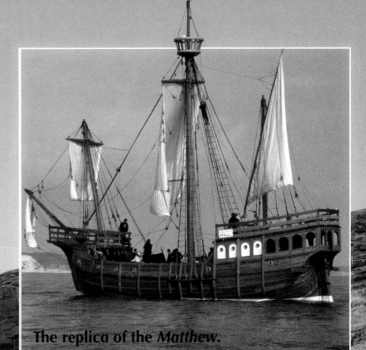

The replica of the *Matthew*.

The *Matthew*

Cabot's boat, the *Matthew,* was a three-masted ship. It weighed about 50 tonnes, making it a relatively small ship. Built of oak, it carried a crew of about 18 sailors and, although small, was very seaworthy. In 1997 a replica was built in Bristol to celebrate the 500th anniversary of the *Matthew*'s voyage.

Timeline

1494 or 1495
Cabot settles in Bristol

May 1497
Cabot sails west

24 June 1497
Makes landfall in either Newfoundland or Nova Scotia

6 August 1497
Returns to Bristol

May 1498
Cabot sets out on his second voyage and is never heard of again

What Next?

Cabot thought he had landed on an island off the coast of Asia. By 1502 it was called "the new found land", and the name is still used for the Canadian province of Newfoundland.

Naming the continent

Columbus was convinced he had sailed to the "Indies" or Asia, but others were unsure as the land was too close to Europe to be Asia. It was in fact a new continent previously unknown to Europeans.

Who was first?

In 1499–1500, four Europeans sailed to South America. Who arrived first is unclear, although many historians credit Pedro Cabral, who sighted Brazil on 22 April 1500. Vicente Pinzón reached the northeast of Brazil, possibly in January 1500. On a third expedition, Alonso de Ojeda explored the Caribbean coast, and Amerigo Vespucci sailed along the coast further east.

Amerigo Vespucci

Amerigo Vespucci (1451–1512) was born in Florence in northern Italy. In 1491 Vespucci left for Seville in Spain, and in 1499, he joined the expedition led by Alonso de Ojeda (c.1468–1515).

Timeline

1499–1500
Ojeda sails along the Caribbean coast; Vespucci explores eastern Brazil

1500
Vicente Pinzón and Pedro Cabral land in Brazil

1501–02
Vespucci makes second voyage possibly reaching as far south as Patagonia in modern-day Argentina

What Next?

Portugal's territory in the new continent was named 'Brasil', after a term used by Irish monks and seafarers for a legendary unknown land.

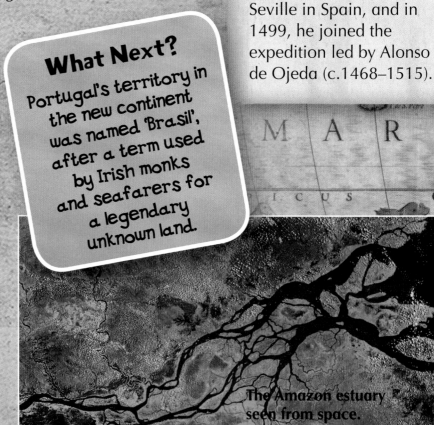

The Amazon estuary seen from space.

Amerigo's land

In 1501–02, Vespucci made a second voyage down the east coast of South America. He was convinced that this was a new continent, which he called the New World. His account of his travels was hugely popular, and his new world was known as "the land of Amerigo", or America (a term initially applied only to South America).

Mercator's map of 1538, the first to name both American continents. It shows North and South America, with the Atlantic Ocean to the east and the Pacific Ocean to the west.

Father of Brazil

Pedro Cabral (c.1467–c.1520) "accidentally discovered" Brazil in April 1500. Whether he was the first European or not, Brazilians celebrate Cabral as the discoverer of their country.

Cabral's caravel.

The Amazon

As Vicente Pinzón (1463–1514) headed northeast up the coast of Brazil, he noticed that the water had changed colour and was no longer salty. He had discovered the estuary of the mighty River Amazon.

East coasting

As Central America was explored, it soon became clear that there was no way through to Asia. But determined explorers continued to search for a passage to China and the east.

Under the French king

King Francis I of France asked Giovanni da Verrazano to explore the coastline of North America between Florida (claimed by Spain) and Newfoundland (claimed by England). Verrazano set out to find land to settle while still searching for a route to China.

Giovanni da Verrazano

Verrazano (c.1485–c.1528) was born in Italy but moved to Dieppe, France, to pursue a naval career. He made several voyages on behalf of the French king. He also became a successful corsair (pirate), raiding Spanish treasure ships returning from Central America.

It's Amazing!

Of Verrazano's four ships, only *La Dauphine* made the entire voyage. Two ships were wrecked. The third returned to France laden with captured Spanish treasure.

Verrazano traded with the Narragansett, whom he described as "the goodliest people".

Chesapeake Bay, Virginia.

Chesapeake Bay

Verrazano mistook the vast inlet of Chesapeake Bay for "a strait through to the Eastern Ocean (Pacific)". He called it the Verrazano Sea. His mistake was only pointed out a century later.

Timeline

1524
Verrazano sets off for the New World with four ships; two are soon wrecked

1 March 1524
Arrives off Cape Fear, North Carolina

April 1524
Enters Chesapeake Bay

17 April 1524
Discovers New York Bay and then sails on to Narragansett Bay, where he spends two weeks exploring

5 May 1524
Sails for Cape Cod and on to Newfoundland

8 July 1524
Returns home to Dieppe

Mission accomplished?

Verrazano arrived off Cape Fear in North Carolina in March 1524. He sailed north to Chesapeake Bay, and then up the Delaware and New Jersey coasts to Rhode Island. Here he spent two weeks in Narragansett Bay, trading with the local population. He continued up the coast to Newfoundland before sailing home across the North Atlantic. He believed he had found a sea route to Asia, and rich land on which to settle.

New York Harbour

As Verrazano sailed up the Atlantic coast, he discovered New York Bay. He anchored in the narrow entrance that today bears his name. He described the upper bay as a "pleasant lake" and named it Santa Margarita in honour of the king's sister.

The Verrazano-Narrows Bridge now stands at the mouth of New York Bay.

The search for the northwest passage

By the middle of the 16th century, it was clear to European explorers that the American continent blocked the sea route west from Europe to Asia. The British attempted to sail through the northwest passage at the very top.

Ocean to ocean

The northwest passage starts in the North Atlantic Ocean and passes between Canada and Greenland into the Arctic Ocean. It then weaves its way between the various islands to the north of Canada before passing round Alaska into the Bering Sea and the northern Pacific Ocean. The main problem with this route is that it is ice-bound for much of the year.

Martin Frobisher

The English adventurer Martin Frobisher (1539–94) first went to sea aged 13. His first voyage was a commercial expedition to Guinea in Africa. He soon became wealthy from piracy, seizing both Spanish and French ships.

An unfortunate hostage

Frobisher met some local Inuit in what is now Frobisher Bay. When five crew members disappeared, he accused the Inuit of kidnapping them and seized an Inuit to bargain with. When this got no response, he brought the Inuit and his canoe back to England. Sadly, the Inuit soon died of a cold.

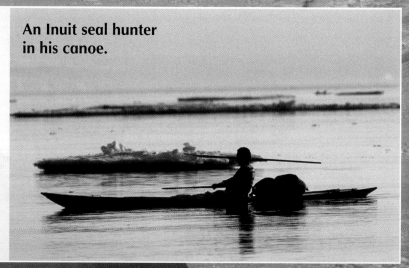

An Inuit seal hunter in his canoe.

What Next?

In 1585, the English explorer John Davis made the first of three voyages to explore the northwest passage. He decided that there was no way through.

Fool's gold

The glittering rock that Frobisher discovered was brought back to England. He formed a company to exploit the mineral. But the 'gold' was in fact pyrite, a yellow, shiny mineral known as fool's gold. The company soon went bankrupt.

Fool's gold, made of sulphur, is used to make sulphuric acid.

A foolish mistake

In 1576 Martin Frobisher sailed from England past Iceland and Greenland across the Davis Strait to the south of Baffin Island. Here he found an inlet – later named Frobisher Bay – around which lived Inuit, who he thought were Chinese. He then discovered glittering rocks he mistook for gold. Frobisher thought he had landed in Asia and found vast wealth, so he abandoned his quest, loaded up his ship with rocks and returned home.

An Inuit igloo near Frobisher Bay.

Timeline

June 1576
Frobisher leaves the Shetland Isles

July 1576
Almost loses his ship, the *Gabriel*, in a storm off Greenland

11 August 1576
Reaches Baffin Island; seizes an Inuit as a hostage

August 1576
Returns to England

1577
Sails to Frobisher Bay again and returns with 200 tonnes of 'gold'

1578
Leads a fleet of 15 ships via Greenland and finds the strait that leads into Hudson Bay

Henry Hudson's tragic voyage

One man, Henry Hudson (1570–1611), was obsessed with finding a northern route from Europe to Asia. He made four voyages in total, exploring both the northwest passage and the Arctic Ocean. He did not succeed, but a famous river, bay and strait are all named after him.

What Next?

In 1670 Prince Rupert, cousin of Charles II of England, set up the Hudson's Bay Company to administer lands around Hudson Bay and develop its fur trade. The company was hugely successful.

Greenland

Hudson Bay

Labrador Sea

North America

→ 1607 journey
→ 1608 journey
→ 1609 journey
→ 1610 journey

Atlantic Ocean

North and east

In 1607 the English Muscovy Company asked Henry Hudson to find a route across the North Pole to China. He sailed north up the coast of Greenland but polar ice stopped him. The following year, he headed along the north coast of Russia, again with no success.

East and west

In 1609 Hudson again searched for a northeast passage. He sailed round Scandinavia but then, with his crew close to mutiny, he turned round and sailed across the Atlantic, along the American coastline in search of a passage to Asia. The next year he set out to find the northwest passage.

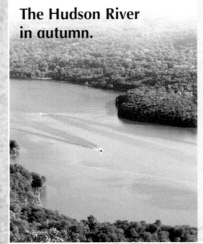

The Hudson River in autumn.

The Hudson River

On 3 September 1609 Henry Hudson sailed into New York Bay. He sailed up the river as far as Albany, only to discover that what he hoped might be a northwest passage was in fact merely a river.

Svalbard

Novaya Zemlya

Iceland

Finland

Sweden

Norway

Amsterdam

London

Europe

Henry Hudson and his son, cast adrift in Hudson Bay.

Cast adrift

On his final voyage, Hudson's ship became trapped in ice in what is now known as Hudson Bay. He was forced to spend the winter there. In spring his crew mutinied and set Hudson, his son and seven loyal sailors adrift in a small boat. Their fate is unknown.

Timeline

1607
Hudson searches for a route across the North Pole to China, and is stopped by ice

1608
Hudson fails to find a northeast passage round Russia

1609
Hudson heads west after his crew mutinies on a voyage east

1610
Hudson searches for a northwest passage; he finds the bay that now bears his name, but is forced to winter in the bay when it freezes

1611
After a mutiny, Hudson is cast adrift and dies

The fatal expedition

The quest for a northwest passage from Europe to Asia continued during the 18th and 19th centuries, but ice around the Arctic islands remained solid almost year round. In 1845, the British Navy sent a major expedition to settle the matter.

John Franklin

Sir John Franklin (1786–1847) was past retirement age when he led his polar expedition. He was, however, vastly experienced. A veteran of two previous Arctic voyages, he was well qualified to lead a major expedition.

Frozen ice

The expedition was led by Sir John Franklin, an experienced explorer. His fleet sailed up Baffin Bay between Greenland and Canada and then headed west through Lancaster Sound at the top of Baffin Island. Here he was iced in and forced to stay put for the winter.

Franklin's crews attempt to free their ice-bound ships.

King William Island

In 1857 Francis McClintock led a search for Franklin on board the *Fox*. On King William Island, they found a tin cylinder buried in a mound of stones. Inside the tin was a document that explained what had happened to Franklin and his team.

Reindeer, a source of meat in summer on King William Island.

Timeline

May 1845
Franklin's expedition leaves England

1846–47
Expedition trapped in ice by King William Island and spends second Arctic winter there

1847
Franklin dies

1848
Remaining members of expedition walk south but die en route

Death on the ice

The next year, 1846, the expedition headed south to avoid the pack-ice, finally reaching clear water near King William Island. Once again, however, the pack-ice closed in, and Franklin and his team were forced to spend another winter in the Arctic. This time they did not survive, but died one by one from exposure.

What Next?

At least 40 expeditions searched for Franklin. Even more men and ships were lost looking for him than were lost in the expedition itself.

Franklin's last note

This note, found by the search mission of 1857, was signed by two of Franklin's officers. It records Franklin's death on 11 June 1847 and the fact that, after the expedition's two ships had been stuck in ice for over a year, the crews had abandoned ship and tried to reach safety by travelling south overland during 1848. None of them survived the journey.

Success at last

The numerous rescue missions that set out to find Franklin produced enough information to map the entire northwest passage. The Suez Canal opened in 1869, allowing ships to travel quickly between Europe and Asia. But one man still wanted to conquer the northwest passage.

Roald Amundsen

When he was just 15, Roald Amundsen (1872–1928) decided to become a polar explorer. He was the first person to sail through the northwest passage and the first to reach the South Pole.

Following Franklin

In 1903 Norwegian explorer Roald Amundsen decided to sail the passage, if only to prove it could be done. He sailed with a crew of only six but enough provisions to last for five years. He followed Sir John Franklin's route, even staying at one of his camps. The team then spent two winters on King William Island, before setting off again in August 1905.

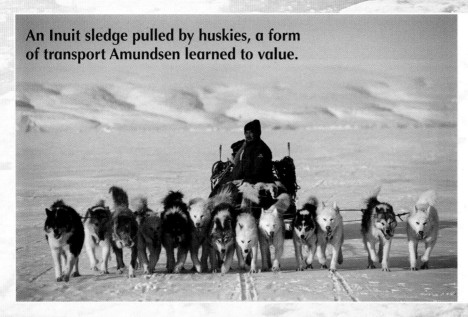

An Inuit sledge pulled by huskies, a form of transport Amundsen learned to value.

Help from the locals

During their three winters in the Arctic, Amundsen and his team learned much from the local Inuit people. Lessons included how to handle dog sledges, how to catch fish and other food, and most importantly, how to survive the intense cold. During their third winter, the team received help from American whalers.

Timeline

June 1903
Amundsen sails from Oslo on the *Gjøa*

August 1903
Reaches Franklin's camp off Erebus Bay

September 1903
Makes camp on King William Island and spends two winters there

August 1905
Sets sail east towards the Beaufort Sea

September 1905
As the ice closes in, forced to spend another winter in the Arctic

October 1906
After breaking free of the ice, the *Gjøa* reaches San Francisco

What Next?

Global warming has caused the ice to recede dramatically. In 2007, this thaw fully opened up the northwest passage for the first time.

Patience is rewarded

As Amundsen sailed between King William Island and the mainland towards the Barents Sea, he met a ship from the Bering Strait sailing east, towards him. Success was almost at hand, but the ice soon closed in again and the team had to spend a third winter in the Arctic. The next year, Amundsen set off again, arriving to a hero's welcome in San Francisco. The northwest passage from the Atlantic to the Pacific Oceans had been conquered.

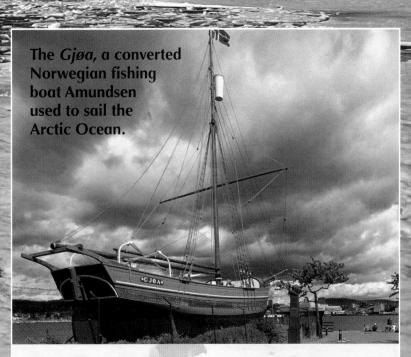

The *Gjøa*, a converted Norwegian fishing boat Amundsen used to sail the Arctic Ocean.

The Arctic Ocean

The ice-cap that covers most of the Arctic Ocean grows bigger during the winter and recedes during the summer. However, the old theory that 24-hour summer sunshine might melt the ice was wrong. The Sun's warming rays are reflected back by the white ice, keeping the Arctic Ocean permanently frozen around the North Pole.

The northeast passage

Like its northwest equivalent, no-one was sure if the northeast passage around the top of Russia existed, and if it did, whether ice always blocked the route. During the 16th century, English and Dutch ships explored the north Russian coast.

Opening up Russia

The first people to explore this route were the English. In 1553 three ships sailed north to find a new route to China. Two became trapped in ice and the entire crew died. The other, commanded by Richard Chancellor (c.1520–56), failed to reach China but did sail into the White Sea to Archangel. From there he travelled overland to Moscow, capital of Ivan the Terrible's Russia.

Spitsbergen, discovered by Barents, became a lucrative source of whales, walruses and seals.

What Next?

Chancellor's journey to Moscow opened up trade between England and Russia. In 1557, The Muscovy Company sent a mission to the Caspian Sea, establishing trade links between England and Persia.

Ivan the Terrible, seated centre, welcomes an English trader to his court.

Ivan the Terrible

Ivan the Terrible (1530–84) was the first ruler to take the title Tsar or emperor of Russia. His Russian nickname *grozny* better translates as 'awe-inspiring' rather than 'terrible', but he did have a violent, unpredictable nature. Ivan did much to expand Russian territory and introduced a number of reforms.

Timeline

1553
Three ships leave England to find a northeast passage to China; two ships are lost

1554
Richard Chancellor treks overland to Moscow

1594
Barents makes his first voyage to find the northeast passage and reaches Novaya Zemlya

1596
On his third expedition, Barents discovers Spitsbergen; he is iced in for the winter

June 1597
Barents dies just as the ice is beginning to melt; his crew is rescued

The hut Barents and his crew built from the wreck of their ship.

Barents' hut

In August 1596, Barents' ship was iced in and crushed. The crew used the timbers to build a cabin in which to survive the winter, and as fuel for heating and cooking.

Willem Barents

The Dutch explorer Willem Barents (c.1550–97) made three attempts to find a sea route to China. Twice he reached Novaya Zemlya – a large island stretching from Siberia up into the Arctic Ocean – but was stopped by ice. On his third mission, Barents could see clear water beyond the island but was soon iced in. He died before he could be rescued.

Bear necessities

Barents and his crew saw many new things on their expeditions. On Bear Island to the south of Spitsbergen, they fought a polar bear, and named the island they had discovered after it. They felt ill after eating the bear, so chose not to hunt them. This was just as well as polar bear meat contains potentially deadly levels of vitamin A.

Polar bears were a constant danger to Arctic explorers.

Round Eurasia

Russian exploration of Siberia during the 18th century (see pages 48–51) meant that the Arctic northeast passage was relatively well known by the later 19th century. It just remained for someone to sail it.

(see pages 48–51)

Planning success

Finnish explorer Adolf Nordenskiöld (1832–1901) worked out that the great rivers of Siberia must send enough warmish water north into the Arctic Ocean during the summer months to keep its coastal waters largely free of ice. He hoped to sail through the northeast passage by hugging the coastline.

What Next?

With the construction of powerful icebreakers during the 20th century, the northeast passage has become a major international waterway.

Barents Sea

SWEDEN

FINLAND

NORWAY

RUSSIA

UNITED KINGDOM

⊙ Karlskrona

E U R O P E

FRANCE

ITALY

SPAIN

Mediterranean Sea

ATLANTIC OCEAN

Suez canal

A F R I C A

SAUDI ARABIA

INDIAN OCEAN

The *Vega*, a powerful ice-resistant ship.

The *Vega*

Nordenskiöld's ship, the *Vega*, was a whaling ship. The hull was made of oak and had an outer layer of tougher wood to resist the ice. In addition to her sails, she also had a steam engine.

Success at last

ARCTIC OCEAN

Leaving from southern Sweden on the *Vega*, Nordenskiöld hugged the coast, and was less than 200 kilometres from Cape Dezhnev at the eastern end of Siberia when he was iced in for the winter. When the ice cleared the following summer, he sailed round Asia to circumnavigate the entire Eurasian landmass.

Bering Strait

ASIA

Cape Dezhnev

Bering Sea

Today the Chukchi live in permanent settlements.

The Chukchi

The hardy Chukchi people of northeastern Siberia were traditionally divided into coastal hunters and inland reindeer herders who moved with their herds. The Chukchi helped Nordenskiöld and his men during their winter stay.

CHINA

INDIA

Bay of Bengal

South China Sea

PACIFIC OCEAN

N

W   E

S

INDONESIA

Timeline

June 1878
Vega leaves Karlskrona in southeast Sweden; Nordenskiöld boards in Norway

September 1878
Vega is trapped by ice near Cape Dezhnev and winters there

July 1879
Vega breaks free of the ice and sails south into the Bering Sea

April 1880
After a lengthy voyage across the Pacific and Indian oceans, the *Vega* arrives back in Sweden

Opening up Japan

One of the countries Columbus and other Europeans wanted to reach in Asia was Japan, an island empire lying off the east coast. Yet European contact with the country was limited, and for a long time Japan shut its doors to all foreign visitors.

Religion and trade

The Portuguese first visited Japan in 1542 and were soon followed by the Jesuits. In 1609, the Dutch East India Company established a trading base near Nagasaki. In 1638, following the Shimabara rebellion, a 37,000-strong Japanese Christian army was massacred at Hara castle. Soon after, Portuguese traders were expelled. Only the Dutch and Chinese were allowed to continue to trade with Japan as the country closed itself off from the rest of the world.

Timeline

1542
First Portuguese traders arrive on Tanegashima

1639
Traders expelled from Japan; isolation begins

1853
First visit by US fleet led by Commodore Perry

1854
Perry forces Japan to sign treaty with USA

1867
Japan begins process of modernization

Himeji Castle, in Kansai, has survived Japan's many wars unharmed.

Tokugawa Ieyasu, shogun of Japan.

The English samurai

William Adams (1564–1620) was the first Englishman to visit Japan in 1600. Imprisoned at first, he was later employed by the local lord to help build a modern navy. Made a samurai, or knight, he became a trusted advisor to Tokugawa Ieyasu, the shogun, or leading military ruler of Japan.

Gunboat diplomacy

During the 19th century, the USA became a major Pacific power. In 1853 the US government sent a naval expedition to force the Japanese to negotiate and trade. Led by Commodore Matthew Perry, the fleet entered the port of Uraga in 1853 and returned the following year to Edo Bay with a large squadron of warships. Faced with such military might, the Japanese caved in.

A samurai warrior in full armour.

It's Amazing!

Within 50 years, Japan used western technology to build a navy capable of beating the Russian imperial fleet.

The shogunate

Although Japan was supposedly ruled by its divine emperor, real power lay in the hands of the shogun. These military leaders continued to rule Japan until they were overthrown in 1867–68 and power was given back to the emperor.

The samurai rebels

Restored to power in 1867, the emperor embarked on a process of modernization. Not everybody was happy about this and the samurai warriors of the Satsuma clan were massacred in a battle with the new Japanese army in 1877.

Satsuma rebels surrender to government forces.

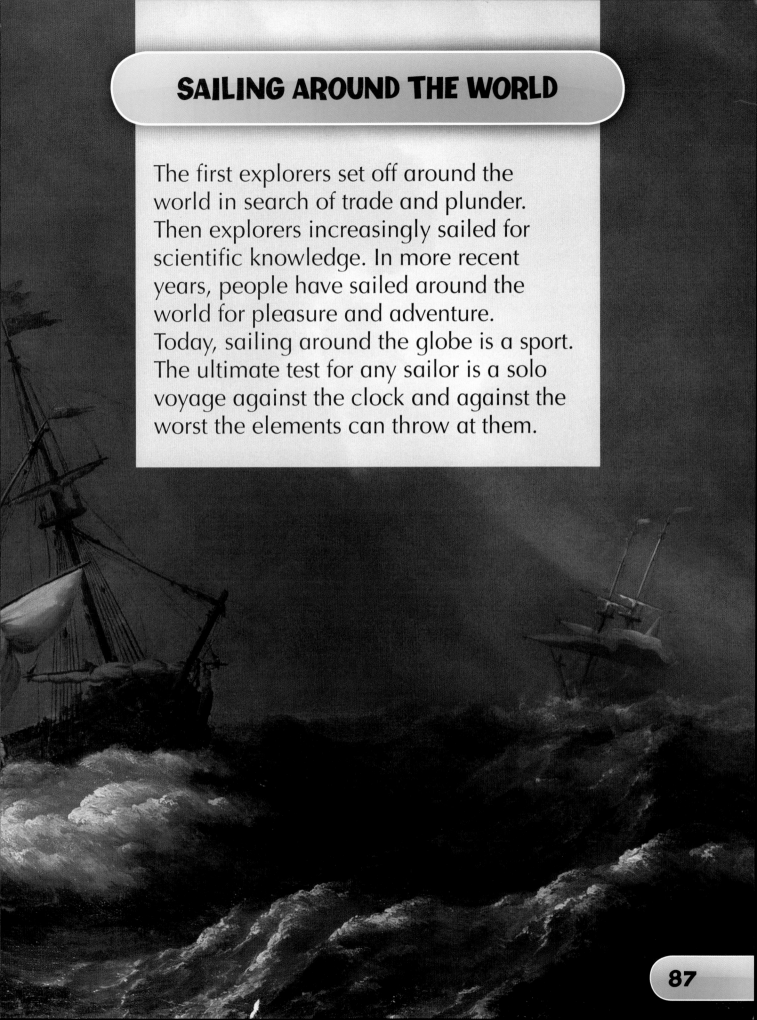

SAILING AROUND THE WORLD

The first explorers set off around the world in search of trade and plunder. Then explorers increasingly sailed for scientific knowledge. In more recent years, people have sailed around the world for pleasure and adventure. Today, sailing around the globe is a sport. The ultimate test for any sailor is a solo voyage against the clock and against the worst the elements can throw at them.

The impossible voyage

Ferdinand Magellan didn't mean to sail round the world, and in fact he didn't, because he died half way round. But his voyage is forever associated with the first circumnavigation of the world, and was a remarkable feat of exploration.

A new route to Asia

Magellan set out to do what Columbus had tried 27 years' earlier – sailing west to find a sea route to Asia. With five Spanish ships, he set out in 1519 in search of the Spice Islands in Indonesia. He sailed south down the Atlantic then wintered in Patagonia (southern Argentina).

An old map showing the Strait of Magellan at the tip of South America, which connects the Atlantic and Pacific oceans.

Ferdinand Magellan

Magellan (c.1480–1521) was born in Portugal. He moved to Spain in 1517 to work for the Spanish king. Magellan was a skilled navigator and leader, demanding much of his men and even more of himself.

Battle of Mactan

In the Philippines, Magellan tried to convert the local chiefs to Christianity. When the chief of Mactan refused, Magellan set out to punish him. Magellan was killed when the chief and his army attacked him and his men.

Magellan was killed by blows to the arm and the right leg.

Guam

The island of Guam is one of the Mariana Islands. The Spanish called these islands the Ladrones, the Spanish word for 'thieves', as the islanders stole everything they could. But they gave Magellan fresh water, coconuts and rice to feed his crew.

Guam is dotted with these 'latte' stones – the remains of ancient houses.

Across the Pacific

Magellan sailed through the strait that now bears his name into the Pacific Ocean. As he crossed the ocean, his fleet ran out of food, but they reached Guam in March 1521. Here they took on provisions and set off for the Philippines, where Magellan hoped to convert the people to Christianity. He was killed the following month.

What Next?

Magellan claimed the Philippines as Spanish territory and they remained so until 1898. The Philippines became the only Christian nation in Asia.

Timeline

10 September 1519
Magellan sets sail from Spain with five ships

March/April 1520
Winters in Patagonia and puts down a revolt by one his captains

November 1520
Sails through the Strait of Magellan into the Pacific Ocean

6 March 1521
Reaches Guam

16 March 1521
Arrives in the Philippines

28 March 1521
Magellan's servant talks to the locals in his own language, proving to Magellan that he had reached Asia

27 April 1521
Magellan killed on Mactan Island

89

The voyage home

Soon after Magellan's death, the remaining voyagers elected João Lopes Carvalho as their leader. Carvalho burned one of the three ships, destroyed Magellan's records, and for the next four months raided any passing ship for booty.

The *Victoria*, the only ship to make it home.

The new leader

Juan Sebastián Delcano (c.1492–1526) was the Basque seaman who completed Magellan's voyage. He showed that travellers who sailed west round the world lost a day by the time they came home, due to the rotation of the Earth.

Homeward bound

When Carvalho failed to find the Spice Islands, command was given to Juan Delcano. He discovered the spice-rich islands and then sailed home west to Spain. On board the *Victoria*, Delcano reached Spain in September 1522. With him were only 17 out of the original 250 European men, as well as four East Indians.

Atlantic Ocean

EUROPE

Spain

AFRICA

It's a Mystery!

When Magellan came out of the Strait of Magellan into the new ocean, he found it to be "calm and benevolent", so he named it the Pacific Ocean.

Pacific Ocean

SOUTH AMERICA

Strait of Magellan

The great voyage

Although he did not live to enjoy it, Magellan's voyage was a huge achievement. He had discovered a westerly route to Asia and sailed across the Pacific Ocean, showing Europeans just how big the world was. He had also opened up new trade possibilities in the Philippines and Spice Islands, as well as discovering a whole new world of Pacific islands to be explored – and exploited – by Europeans.

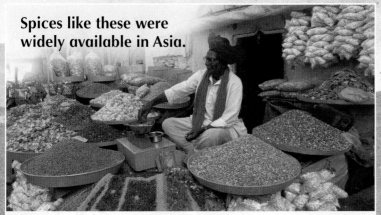

Spices like these were widely available in Asia.

Spice trade

Spices were highly valued in Europe for flavouring meat after it had been salted to preserve it. They were also used to flavour drinks. Among those found in the Spice Islands were pepper, cloves and nutmeg.

Timeline

May 1521
Carvalho is elected leader a few days after Magellan is killed in battle

October 1521
After failing to find the Spice Islands, the remaining crew get rid of Carvalho and give command to Delcano

November 1521
Delcano finds the Spice Islands and sails for home in the *Victoria*, leaving the *Trinidad* behind for repairs

April 1522
The *Trinidad* returns to the Spice Islands and is held captive by the Portuguese

6 September 1522
Delcano reaches Spain

Indian Ocean

Pacific Ocean

Magellan killed

Philippines

Spice Islands

Southern Ocean

The pirate adventurer

After the successful voyage of Magellan and Delcano, ships sailed to the Philippines and Spice Islands, but none circumnavigated the world. An English adventurer and pirate, Francis Drake, was the next to attempt such a voyage in 1577, sponsored by Queen Elizabeth I.

Raiding the Spanish

As relations between England and Spain grew hostile in the 1570s, Francis Drake planned to attack the Spanish in the Pacific Ocean. In 1577 he set sail with five ships. He raided Spanish treasure ships in the Pacific, capturing 80 pounds of gold.

A replica of the *Golden Hind* built in 1977 to mark the 400th anniversary of Drake's voyage.

Francis Drake

Drake (c.1540–96) was born in Tavistock, Devon. He was a skilled navigator and seaman and England's most famous pirate. He played a key role in defeating the Spanish Armada in 1588.

The Atlantic slave trade

Francis Drake's relative John Hawkins took slaves from West Africa to the West Indies. He sold them for goods he then sold in England. In 1566 Drake took part in one such voyage, narrowly escaping when the Spanish attacked.

Slaves were transported in neck irons. Many died on the way.

A wealthy return

By now reduced to just his flagship, the *Golden Hind*, Drake stopped for repairs just north of modern-day San Francisco. He claimed the area for England. He then crossed the Pacific Ocean to the Spice Islands, where he loaded up with spices. He sailed for home with a huge treasure.

Elizabeth I knights Drake on board his ship.

Arise, Sir Francis

When Drake returned home in 1580, Queen Elizabeth I did not acknowledge his achievement, as she did not want to upset the Spanish. However she soon changed her mind, threw a banquet on board the *Golden Hind* and knighted Francis Drake.

Timeline

13 December 1577
Drake leaves Plymouth with five ships

April 1578
Sails past eastern Brazil

24 August 1578
Reaches Strait of Magellan

7 September 1578
Reaches the Pacific, but is forced to sail about 160 km south of Cape Horn

June 1579
Sails as far north as Vancouver Island

25 July 1579
Starts voyage across the Pacific

26 September 1580
Arrives home in Plymouth

Sailing with Drake

John Herbert sailed with Drake around the world. Here is his account of the voyage.

The voyage south

23 MAY 1578 I sail on board the Pelican with Master Drake, a skilled seaman from my county of Devon. He has been commanded by our majesty, Queen Elizabeth, to attack the Spanish, but he did not tell us we were bound for the Pacific Ocean until we were well at sea. Our fleet has lost two ships already in the South Atlantic, and the Mary was abandoned because it was found to be full of rot.

21 AUGUST 1578 Our three ships passed through the Strait of Magellan and into the Pacific. A mighty gale blew us far south and east, so that we sailed back into the Atlantic. And so we proved that these two oceans meet at the far south.

Our master has renamed the Pelican the Golden Hind, in honour of his patron, Sir Christopher Hatton. There is a hind (deer) on Sir Christopher's coat of arms.

Raiding the seas

NOVEMBER 1578 We are now on our own in the Golden Hind, as we have lost a ship to the storm and the Elizabeth has returned home. But we are rich, for twice we have seized ships of Spain, and have raided their towns on the shore. We gave chase to the Cacafuego bound for Panama, and took 80 pounds of gold including a crucifix of solid gold, as well as 13 chests full of gold bullion and much silver and jewels.

17 JUNE 1579 We landed today in a place we do not know, but there are no Spanish here to detain us. Master Drake has claimed the land for the crown of England, and has named it Nova Albion for New Britain. The native people are friendly, and we plan to stay here to repair our ships. From here we will head north again to search for a passage round this land to the Atlantic Ocean. Then, I hope, we will return home at last.

Arctic Ocean

NORTH AMERICA

Atlantic Ocean

ASIA

Pacific Ocean

AFRICA

SOUTH AMERICA

Indian Ocean

AUSTRALIA

ANTARCTICA

Round and round and round the world

After Drake, the number of people circumnavigating the globe remained very small. The Englishman Thomas Cavendish completed the voyage in 1586–88, as did a few unknown traders and pirates. But William Dampier sailed round the world not once but three times.

Raiding and exploring

William Dampier was an adventurer. In the 1670s he joined a pirate ship. He worked in a logging camp on the Gulf of Mexico, but lost his fortune when a hurricane destroyed the timber. He sailed up and down the Pacific coast raiding Spanish ships, and in 1686 guided a ship across the Pacific. Dampier then sailed south to the northwest coast of New Holland (as Australia was then called), before returning to England in 1691.

Timeline

1676
Dampier joins a logging camp in Gulf of Mexico

1677–78
Starts raiding Spanish shipping and settlements

1686
Crosses the Pacific

1688
Lands in Australia

1691
Returns to England

1699–1701
Commands HMS *Roebuck* and is shipwrecked

1703–07
Sails round the world as a pirate

1708–10
Completes third circumnavigation

William Dampier

William Dampier (c.1651–1715) was born in East Coker, Somerset, and went to sea as a young man. He was a skilled seaman but also a keen observer of new lands, flora and fauna, as well as winds, tides and currents. He became a pirate, but said he did so "more to indulge my curiosity than to get wealth".

Round twice more

In 1703 Dampier set out again, this time as a licensed pirate. He was less successful than before, letting a Spanish treasure galleon slip away. He was jailed in the Dutch East Indies for piracy, and only returned home in 1707. A year later he set out again, this time as a pilot on two pirate ships. They roamed the Pacific Ocean with great success, although Dampier received little reward for his efforts.

The northwest coast of Australia, twice visited by William Dampier.

Some of the many drawings of animals and plants in Dampier's books.

Dampier's account

Dampier wrote a book about his adventures. *A New Voyage Round the World* was published in 1697 and became a bestseller. Other books followed, with many valuable charts and surveys about the Pacific Ocean.

There is very little life on the rocky Ascension Island, but green turtles like this one lay their eggs there.

Ascension Island

In 1698 Dampier commanded HMS *Roebuck* on an expedition to find the supposed southern continent. On his way home, he was shipwrecked on Ascension Island in the Atlantic and stuck there for five weeks before he and his crew were rescued.

It's Amazing!

In 1704, Dampier fell out with one of his crew, Alexander Selkirk, and left him on an uninhabited island near Chile. Dampier's ship rescued him in 1709. Selkirk's adventures were the inspiration for Daniel Defoe's Robinson Crusoe.

Press gangs

In the 18th century, roughly one third of all men in the British Royal Navy had been forced into service by naval press-gangs, which were authorized to force men into going to sea. Among Anson's crew were pensioners drafted into naval service.

A man is dragged off by a press gang.

George Anson

Many of those who had circumnavigated the world in the 16th and 17th centuries were adventurers or pirates. George Anson was a naval commander acting on British government orders.

Attacking the Spanish

In 1740 Britain and Spain were at war. The British government ordered Anson to sail with seven ships to raid Spanish settlements on the Pacific coast of South America. Three of his ships were lost or turned back before he reached Cape Horn but Anson continued into the Pacific Ocean, inflicting great damage on Spanish shipping in the region.

What Next?

Anson became head of the navy. He reformed discipline, reduced corruption and raised naval standards.

The ruins of St Paul's cathedral in Macao, a Portuguese colony from 1557 to 1999.

Sealing his fortune

After capturing 32 wagonloads of treasure from *Nuestra Señora de Covadonga* in 1743, Anson needed somewhere to sell it. He chose the Portuguese colony of Macao, where he sold the booty to Chinese traders. Anson returned home a very rich man.

Anson's flagship the *Centurion* (left) attacks a Spanish treasure ship.

Golden success

With his own ships damaged, Anson then consolidated all his crew onto one ship – his flagship *Centurion* – and crossed the Pacific to Macao on the Chinese coast. From here, he sailed out to capture a Spanish treasure galleon, *Nuestra Señora de Covadonga,* as it sailed from the Philippines to Mexico, seizing its booty.

Drawing the journey

Brett made drawings of sea lions like these.

Piercy Brett, a lieutenant with Anson, kept a record of their journey by making drawings of what they saw. He drew many of the animals that they encountered along the way.

Timeline

18 September 1740
Anson leaves England with seven ships

June 1741
Reaches Juan Fernández Islands off Chile with just four ships

1742
Reaches Macao with only one ship

20 June 1743
Captures *Nuestra Señora de Covadonga* off the Philippines

1744
Returns to England

John Byron, the record breaker

John Byron entered the record books when he completed the fastest circumnavigation yet recorded, sailing round the world in less than two years. However, that was not what he set out to do, so his voyage was considered a failure at the time.

Disobeying orders

Byron was put in command of a naval voyage to find and claim new lands in the South Atlantic. He set sail in 1764 on board the *Dolphin*, and reached the Falkland Islands. He then entered the Pacific but instead of obeying orders to sail north, he sailed west.

Northern Mariana Islands

Gilbert Islands (Kiribati)

Batavia (Jakarta)

Tokelau

Indian Ocean

Australia

N
NW   NE
W   E
SW   SE
S

John Byron

British-born Byron (1723–86) joined the navy in his teens. He served under George Anson and fought the French in 1758. After his circumnavigation, he became governor of Newfoundland.

King penguins, one of five species of penguin on the Falkland Islands.

New claims

Byron claimed the Falkland Islands in the South Atlantic for Britain. He also claimed islands he found in the Pacific. He failed to anchor in one group of Tuamotu islands, which he named the Disappointment Islands. He named an island in the Gilbert Islands after himself!

Timeline

21 June 1764
Byron leaves Plymouth

1765
Reaches the Falkland Islands and claims them for Britain just as a French fleet claims them for France

April 1765
Enters the Pacific and discovers the Tuamotu, Tokelau and Gilbert (now Kiribati) islands

November 1765
Reaches Batavia, now called Jakarta

9 May 1766
Returns to Plymouth after a voyage lasting 22 months, 18 days

Fast passage home

When he reached Batavia (now Jakarta) in Indonesia, Byron decided to head straight for home. He made a quick passage to Cape Town and sped up the Atlantic for Britain, which he reached in May 1766. He had set a world record and found islands in the Pacific, but had found no new Atlantic lands or any sea passages.

South America

South Atlantic Ocean

Tuamotu Islands

Pacific Ocean

Falkland Islands

New colonies

In 1763 France lost its American and Indian empires to Britain. The French government decided to send a naval expedition to the South Seas to find new lands to colonize.

The South Seas

The expedition, led by Louis-Antoine de Bougainville, arrived in the South Pacific in 1768. Bougainville claimed the Tuamotu Islands for France and then sailed on to Tahiti, which he also claimed. Here he took on board Ahu-toru, a chieftain's son who wanted to visit France. Laden with new supplies, Bougainville sailed west through the Society Islands, Samoa and the New Hebrides (now Vanuatu).

Timeline

January 1768
Bougainville's two ships pass through the Strait of Magellan into the Pacific Ocean

March 1768
Claims the Tuamotu islands for France

April 1768
Sails into Tahiti

4 June 1768
Avoids shipwreck on the Great Barrier Reef

September 1768
Sails to Batavia

16 March 1769
Arrives home in St Malo

It's Amazing!

During the voyage, it was discovered that one of the crew, the servant, Jeanne Baré, was in fact a woman disguised as a man.

Louis-Antoine de Bougainville

Bougainville (1729–1811) studied law and mathematics before going to sea. He served in Canada as aide-de-camp to General Montcalm, who lost Quebec to the British in 1759, when he organized the evacuation of French troops. After his circumnavigation, he served as secretary to King Louis XV.

Missed opportunity

Bougainville rounded the Great Barrier Reef off Australia – missing the chance to claim the continent for France – and headed to the Dutch East Indies. He replenished his supplies and sailed across the Indian Ocean and back home to France. He had lost only seven out of more than 200 men (and one woman) while at sea.

A boat race in Tahiti, which Bougainville considered paradise.

The Great Barrier Reef

The Great Barrier Reef runs down the northeast coast of Australia. Its coral islands and reefs prevent easy access to the coast. Had Bougainville found a way through, Australia might have become a French, not British colony.

The beautiful coral of the Great Barrier Reef, which is a danger to ships.

Bougainvillea

Among the crew was botanist Philibert Commerçon, who recorded many new species. Among them was Bougainvillea, a brightly flowered tropical vine introduced to Europe by Bougainville and named after him.

Bougainvillea, a pretty vine from South America.

America does it

Charles Wilkes was the first American to circumnavigate the globe. Along the way, he contributed to a vast increase in understanding of the world's seas.

Sailing the oceans

In 1838 Wilkes was put in charge of the US South Seas Exploring Expedition, designed to increase scientific and maritime knowledge. The fleet of six ships sailed south to Tierra del Fuego and on to the Antarctic. From there it sailed across the Pacific to Australia, back to the Antarctic and then north via Hawaii to Oregon. It crossed the Pacific again to the East Indies, sailed across the Indian Ocean and round the Cape of Good Hope, arriving in New York in 1842.

Timeline

18 August 1838
Expedition departs and crosses the Atlantic

February 1839
Establishes a base on Tierra del Fuego

November 1839
Crosses the Pacific to Australia

19 January 1840
First sights Antarctica

September 1840
Studies volcanoes in Hawaii

April 1841
Sails to Oregon coast

November 1841
Sails for home

9 August 1842
Three remaining ships arrive in New York

Wilkes braved icebergs like this to land on Antarctica and take rock samples.

Charles Wilkes

Charles Wilkes (1798–1877), from New York City, joined the US navy at the age of 18. He became interested in astronomy and surveying and an authority in hydrography – the science of the oceans, seas, lakes and rivers. After the expedition ended, he prepared its many papers for publication.

The achievement

Wilkes's fleet sailed more than 128,000 kilometres and crossed the Pacific three times. It mapped the Oregon coast and 2560 kilometres of the Antarctic coastline, surveyed more than 300 islands and produced 180 navigational charts. His achievements proved that the USA could mount an expedition comparable in size and ambition to those of Britain and France.

The guanaco, one of the animals on Tierra del Fuego.

What Next?

Wilkes's charting of the Oregon coastline and the Columbia River increased American interest in Oregon, at the time jointly run with Britain. In 1846 the territory became part of the USA.

Tierra del Fuego

Wilkes's naturalists observed many animals on Tierra del Fuego, the island at the southern tip of South America. These included Magellan penguins and plovers, seals, wolves, guanacos and foxes.

The three-masted *Vincennes*.

The *Vincennes*

The *Vincennes* was a 780-tonne sloop on which Wilkes spent most of the expedition. He started off with six ships, but most were too old for the expedition. Two were lost near Cape Horn and only half the fleet made it home.

Slocum preferred to sail by himself and wrote a bestseller called Sailing Alone Around the World.

Going solo

By the late 19th century, circumnavigations took place all the time, as steam ships sailed the world carrying tea, coal, wheat and other products. But no one had ever sailed a yacht single-handed round the world. That prize went to a 54-year-old American sea captain.

Setting sail

After three years restoring his small yacht, the *Spray*, Joshua Slocum set sail from Boston, Massachusetts in April 1895 and crossed the Atlantic to Gibraltar. He then sailed south via the Cape Verde Islands to Brazil, spending Christmas in Montevideo. He entered the Pacific Ocean through the Strait of Magellan.

The *Spray*

Slocum's boat, the *Spray,* was an ancient oysterman he first saw propped up in a field and covered with canvas. During 1893, he completely rebuilt her hull using white pasture oak. She was only 11.2 m long and 4.3 m wide, but was very seaworthy and easy to sail single-handed.

A short cut

The opening of the Suez Canal in 1869 meant there was no need for yachts to sail round the Cape of Good Hope. Joshua Slocum did not take this route, however, choosing instead to spend the Christmas of 1897 in South Africa.

A steam ship passes through the Suez Canal.

Alone round the world

Slocum crossed the Pacific to Australia, where he spent some months sailing slowly down the east coast. He then headed north round the top of Australia and crossed the Indian Ocean to Cape Town, where he spent another Christmas. From there, he sailed via St Helena and Ascension to northern Brazil and up to Rhode Island, arriving in June 1898. He had sailed a total distance of 74,000 kilometres on his own. He wrote a best-selling book about his adventure.

Timeline

24 April 1895
Slocum sets sail from Boston, Massachusetts

July 1895
Crosses the Atlantic to Gibraltar

December 1895
After sailing south, spends Christmas in Uruguay

1896
Cruises through the Pacific to Australia

1897
Cruises from Australia across the Indian Ocean

December 1897
Docks in Cape Town, South Africa

27 June 1898
Arrives in Rhode Island

It's a Mystery!

In 1909 Joshua Slocum set out from Bristol, Rhode Island, bound for Grand Cayman in the Caribbean Sea and was never seen again. It is probable that a steamer ran him down when he was asleep below deck.

Lady Brassey wrote an account of her voyage.

Sailing in style

The first private yacht to circumnavigate the world was the *Sunbeam*, owned and skippered by Thomas Brassey, a British MP and later lord. The voyage lasted from July 1876 to May 1877. Brassey was accompanied by his wife and a crew of 32 that included a maid.

One-stop voyage

Before the 1960s all mariners wishing to sail single-handed round the world had to call in at numerous ports, as sail boats were slow and had to stop for supplies. New technology allowed yachts to sail faster and further than ever.

Gipsy Moth IV on a calm day.

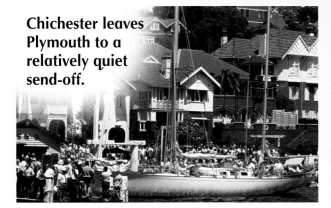

Chichester leaves Plymouth to a relatively quiet send-off.

Leaving home

Francis Chichester left Plymouth harbour in his boat, the *Gipsy Moth IV*, a two-masted ketch. He aimed to better the times achieved by the fastest clipper ships of the 19th century.

The record breaker

Francis Chichester (1901–72) was both a sailor and an aviator – he was the first man to fly solo east–west across the Tasman Sea in 1931. In 1960 he became the first person to sail solo from east to west across the North Atlantic against the prevailing winds, setting a time of 40 days. In 1966, he set out to sail around the world making only one stop.

Alone on board

It takes huge stamina to sail a boat single-handed, as you must always keep a lookout for other boats. Hauling heavy sails or climbing the mast to make repairs requires strength. Loneliness, too, is a great problem.

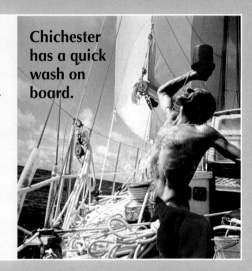

Chichester has a quick wash on board.

Via Sydney to home

The first leg of Chichester's voyage, from Plymouth, England, via the Cape of Good Hope to Sydney, Australia, took 107 days. After a six-week stop in Sydney, Chichester set off across the Pacific Ocean and round Cape Horn into the Atlantic and home to Plymouth. The return leg took 119 days. Chichester had sailed alone round the world in just 226 days at an average speed of 6 knots.

A hero's welcome

Thousands of small boats accompanied *Gipsy Moth IV* into Plymouth Sound on Chichester's return, letting off hooters and sirens while fireboats sprayed red, white and blue water. The Royal Artillery sounded a 10-gun salute. Soon afterwards, he received a knighthood from the Queen.

Sir Francis Chichester on the day he was knighted.

Timeline

27 August 1966
Chichester leaves Plymouth on board *Gipsy Moth IV*

12 December 1966
After 107 days at sea, he arrives in Sydney, where he repairs the yacht and takes on new supplies

29 January 1967
Leaves Sydney

28 May 1967
Returns home to a hero's welcome in Plymouth

7 July 1967
Receives a knighthood from the Queen in Greenwich

Racing around the world

After Francis Chichester's voyage, there was only one yachting record left: sailing single-handed around the world without stopping.

Alone, non-stop

In early 1968 five sailors prepared to face this challenge. The *Sunday Times* newspaper sponsored the race. Each entrant had to start and finish at the same British port of their choosing and sail round the Cape of Good Hope and then Cape Horn. Only one entrant finished: Robin Knox-Johnston became the first person ever to circumnavigate the globe non-stop by himself.

Timeline

14 June 1968
Robin Knox-Johnston leaves Falmouth, England, on board the ketch *Suhaili*

22 April 1969
Knox-Johnston arrives back in Falmouth

2005
Ellen MacArthur sails round the world in *B&Q/Castorama* in a record 71 days

2005
Bruno Peyron and crew in *Orange II* sail round the world in under 51 days

2008
Francis Joyon sets new solo record of 57 days

Robin Knox Johnston

Knox-Johnston (born 1939) was the first person to sail single-handed round the world without stopping. He went round the world again in a crewed yacht in 1977 and won the Jules Verne Trophy for the fastest circumnavigation in 1994.

It's Amazing!

The Jules Verne Trophy is awarded for the fastest circumnavigation of the world. The current record, set by Frenchman Bruno Peyron in 2005, is 50 days, 9 hours, 32 minutes and 45 seconds!

The fastest sailor alive

Solo circumnavigations have always been rare, but for a woman to attempt it is even rarer. British sailor Ellen MacArthur (born in 1976) came second in the Vendée Globe solo round-the-world race in 2001. In 2005, she sailed the trimaran *B&Q/Castorama* solo round the world in 71 days, breaking the record of Frenchman Francis Joyon by one day. Joyon took the record back in 2008, when he completed the voyage in just 57 days.

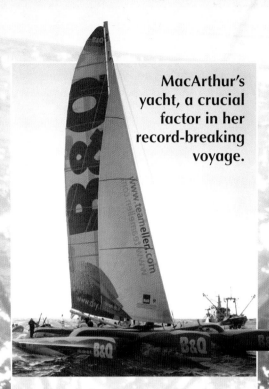

MacArthur's yacht, a crucial factor in her record-breaking voyage.

Ellen MacArthur in training for the 2001 Vendeé Globe race.

Record-breaking boat

The *B&Q/Castorama*, the boat on which Ellen MacArthur set her record, was a high-tech trimaran that was custom-built for her in Australia. Many of its components were designed to be ideally placed for a person of her height.

Natural hazards

Modern yachts use the Global Positioning System, a satellite-based system that tells you where you are. But you still need to keep a look out – it does not tell you that a whale is in your way!

A humpback whale surfaces. Underwater, it is a danger to sailors.

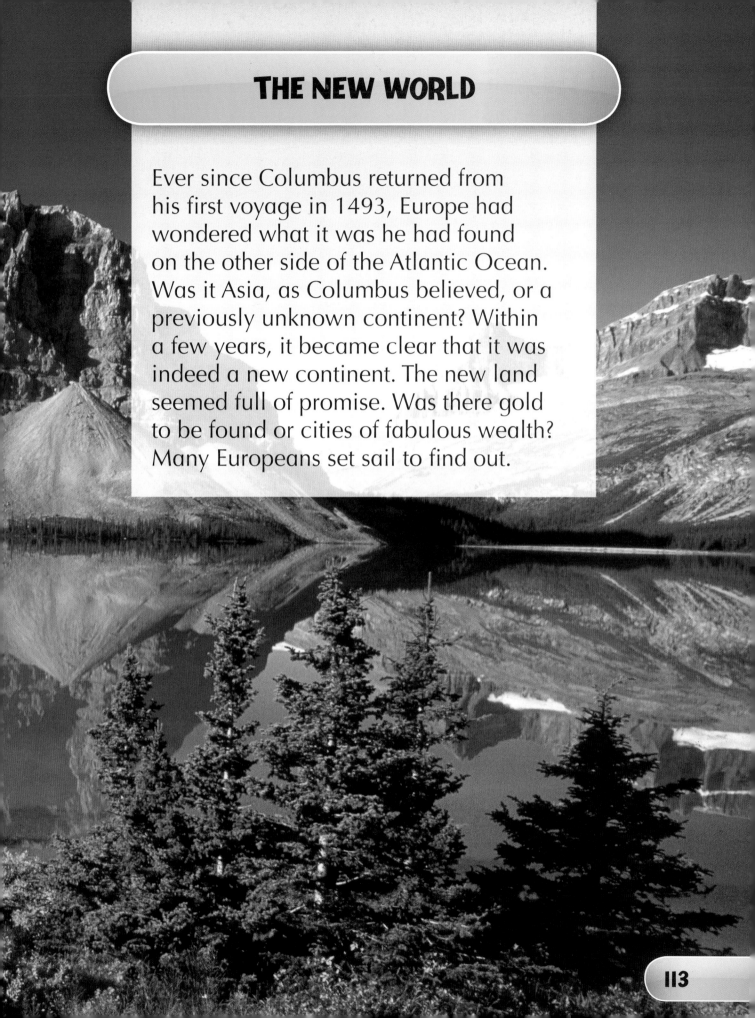

THE NEW WORLD

Ever since Columbus returned from his first voyage in 1493, Europe had wondered what it was he had found on the other side of the Atlantic Ocean. Was it Asia, as Columbus believed, or a previously unknown continent? Within a few years, it became clear that it was indeed a new continent. The new land seemed full of promise. Was there gold to be found or cities of fabulous wealth? Many Europeans set sail to find out.

The return of Columbus

After his first voyage in 1492–93, Columbus crossed the Atlantic three more times to explore the islands he had first visited. These voyages opened up the new continent to European explorers and conquerors.

It's Amazing!

In 1494, Pope Alexander VI signed the Treaty of Tordesillas. He drew a line down a map of the Atlantic Ocean, and divided the new world between the Spanish and Portuguese.

Timeline

1493–96
On his second voyage, Columbus explores and names the Leeward Islands, and establishes a colony on Hispaniola

31 July 1498
On his third voyage, Columbus lands on Trinidad before exploring mainland South America nearby

19 August 1498
Returns to Hispaniola, where he is placed under arrest and then sent home

1502–04
Explores east coast of Central America, searching for a passage to the Indian Ocean

1506
Columbus dies

Round the Caribbean

In 1493–96 Columbus made his second voyage, exploring the Caribbean and establishing a settlement on Hispaniola. On his third voyage in 1498, he became the first European to set foot on South America. He then returned to rule Santo Domingo. Following complaints, he was arrested by the new Spanish governor and sent to Spain for trial.

Caribbean Sea

New settlers

The first Spanish settlements in the New World were established on the island of Hispaniola. The first colony, La Navidad, was destroyed by local Taíno people. Columbus set up a new colony at Santo Domingo, which is now the capital of the Dominican Republic.

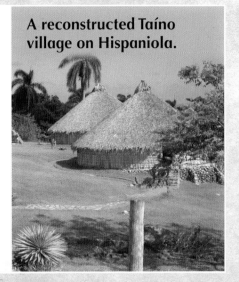

A reconstructed Taíno village on Hispaniola.

Further west

Columbus won his trial in Spain, and in 1502 he set out again. This time he headed west through the islands until he hit land. This was the Central American coastline, but Columbus thought he had found a route through to Asia.

CUBA

La Navidad

North Atlantic Ocean

HISPANIOLA

Santo Domingo

JAMAICA

LEEWARD ISLANDS

 2nd voyage (1493–96)

3rd voyage (1498–1500)

4th voyage (1502–04)

The Spanish Empire

The Spanish were very cruel to the native population, who rebelled against their rule. This, combined with new diseases, totally wiped out the native population of the Caribbean.

Hatuey, a Taíno leader who fought Spanish rule on Cuba and was burnt alive after refusing to be baptized.

TRINIDAD

First steps on the mainland

From their settlements in the Caribbean, the Spanish set out to explore the North and Central American mainland that lay to their west. These explorations opened the way for Spanish colonization of the entire region.

The Pacific

In 1510 the Spanish explorer Vasco Núñez de Balboa (1475–1519) established the Spanish colony of Santa Maria La Antigua del Darien on the Panama isthmus in Central America. Here, he heard reports from the local people of a vast ocean to the west. In 1513 he crossed the isthmus and became the first European to see the Pacific Ocean.

Núñez de Balboa first sets eyes on the Pacific Ocean.

Juan Ponce de León

Juan Ponce de León (c.1460–1521) was an explorer who colonized Puerto Rico and discovered Florida. Rarely for his time, he believed in peaceful colonization. He showed kindness and friendship to the people he met.

It's a Mystery!

The Spanish were keen to explore the islands north of Cuba, which were rumoured to contain a fountain that granted eternal youth if you washed in its waters.

Timeline

1510
Núñez de Balboa establishes first Spanish colony on mainland

March 1513
Ponce de León lands in a place he names Florida

27 September 1513
Núñez de Balboa sights Pacific Ocean and claims it for Spain

1528
Cabeza de Vaca and three others are shipwrecked on the Texas coast, from where they embark on a long journey to safety

1542
Cabeza de Vaca's account of his adventures is published

The long trek

In 1513, Juan Ponce de León sailed north from Spanish Puerto Rico and landed in a place he called Tierra La Florida (Land of Flowers). Fifteen years later, a fleet set out to explore Florida, but was shipwrecked in the Gulf of Mexico. Only a few men survived, among them Álvar Núñez Cabeza de Vaca (c.1490–1556), who wrote about his experiences. Aided by local Yaqui tribesmen, they walked an incredible 2000 km to be rescued.

Yaqui territory

Cabeza de Vaca walked through the region that is now the state of Texas. It was then inhabited by Yaqui and other native peoples. The Spanish conquered the area during the 1600s, and in 1821 it became Mexican territory. Texas declared its independence from Mexico in 1836 and became part of the USA nine years later.

A Yaqui dancer invoking the power of the spirit world.

Bison

While trekking through what is now Texas, Cabeza de Vaca met a group of local people who had gathered to harvest the prickly pear cactus. They also encountered a herd of hairy, hunch-backed cows grazing on the plains – the first bison ever seen by Europeans.

Cortés in Mexico

The people that explorers first encountered in the Americas were self-sufficient farmers and hunters. In European eyes they were very primitive, but this view of the continent changed when the Aztec empire of Mexico was discovered.

Into the interior

In 1518 the Spanish governor of Cuba sent 11 ships under the command of Hernán Cortés (1485–1547) to explore the coast of the Yucatán peninsula of Mexico. Once there, Cortés learned of a great inland empire and set out to find it. He marched inland with only a handful of men and horses, but soon found local allies willing to fight against their rulers, the Aztecs.

An Aztec map of Tenochtitlán.

Tenochtitlán

The Aztec capital housed perhaps 250,000 people – far more than any European city of the time. It ruled an empire of 10 million that stretched from the Pacific to the Caribbean.

An Aztec calendar, based on a complex cycle of 20-day periods.

The Aztecs

The Aztecs settled in central Mexico in the 13th century AD and soon created a powerful empire. They developed a complex calendar and built vast cities of stone. Yet they had no iron tools, wheeled vehicles or horses.

A mighty empire falls

Cortés entered the Aztec capital, Tenochtitlán, and took the emperor, Moctezuma II, hostage. Cortés was then forced to return to the coast to deal with charges of insubordination, and left the city in the charge of his lieutenant Pedro de Alvarado. On his return, Cortés found that Alvarado had massacred a group of Aztec nobles. In response, the Aztecs revolted, killed Moctezuma and forced the Spanish to flee. A year later, Cortés seized Tenochtitlán and took control of the entire Aztec empire.

The city of Tenochtitlán, built on an island in Lake Texcoco.

Moctezuma II

The Aztec emperor Moctezuma II (reigned 1502–20) was portrayed as a weak leader in Spanish accounts. Before losing to Cortés, however, he had many military successes and conquered large parts of southern Mexico.

Timeline

18 November 1518
Cortés leads an expedition from Cuba with 900 men

16 August 1519
Cortés moves inland

November 1519
Cortés enters Tenochtitlán and takes the Aztec emperor, Moctezuma II, hostage

December 1519
The Aztecs revolt when Cortés is out of the city

30 June–1 July 1520
Cortés fights his way out of Tenochtitlán, losing half his men

May–August 1521
The Spanish and their allies attack and seize Tenochtitlán

It's Amazing!
Tenochtitlán was not the first important city in the Valley of Mexico. The great city of Teotihuacán stood nearby many centuries earlier. The huge, sprawling Mexico City stands there today.

In search of the Incas

Rumours circulated in the New World of a gold-rich civilization known as Birù (or Peru) on the Pacific coast of South America. One man set out to look for this legendary civilization.

Francisco Pizarro

Pizarro (c.1475–1541) served as a soldier with Balboa in 1513 before becoming a cattle breeder in Panama. When he set out to conquer the Inca empire in 1530, he was around 55. This was his last chance of glory.

Head for the hills

Spanish explorer Francisco Pizarro led three expeditions to find Birù. The first found nothing. The second, in 1526, sailed as far south as the Inca city of Tumbes in northern Peru. It returned with news of an advanced civilization up in the mountains. Pizarro set out in 1530 to conquer it.

The Inca empire

The Inca empire stretched the length of South America from Ecuador in the north to central Chile in the south and across the Andes to Argentina in the east. The empire was connected by a vast network of paved roads.

An Inca headdress – one of many objects they made from gold.

Third time lucky

Pizarro and his party made their way south to Tumbes, which they now found in ruins following a civil war in the Inca empire. With fewer than 200 men, Pizarro set out to meet the emperor, Atahuallpa. He took the emperor hostage and was offered a room full of gold and silver to release him. But when this treasure was handed over, Pizarro executed the emperor and seized the capital, Cusco. The Inca empire was his.

Machu Picchu, a royal Inca retreat in the mountains of Peru, was abandoned by the Incas after the Spanish conquest and remained unknown to the outside world until 1911.

Timeline

1524–25
Pizarro finds no gold on first voyage south

1526–28
Sails south to Tumbes where he hears of a city in the mountains

May 1532
Returns to Tumbes, which he finds in ruins

November 1532
Heads inland to Cajamarca, where he takes Atahuallpa hostage

July 1533
Atahuallpa is executed

November 1533
Pizarro's army take the Inca capital Cusco

The ruins of Sacsahuamán.

Sacsahuamán fortress

This was the main Inca fortress guarding the capital, Cusco. It was a vast stone building, with three massive terraced walls, capable of housing 5000 soldiers. Inca stonemasons cut and shaped each stone individually.

What Next?
The last Inca stronghold fell to the Spanish in 1572, but the edges of the empire remained largely unconquered until the early 1800s.

In search of gold

Spanish explorers obsessively searched for gold. They rarely found what they were looking for, and many lost their lives. They did, however, open up the interior of the continent for further exploration.

It's Amazing!

In 1539, de Soto came across Juan Ortiz, a survivor of the 1528 expedition. Ortiz joined de Soto's expedition as an interpreter.

Timeline

May 1539
De Soto lands in Tampa Bay, Florida

1539–41
De Soto heads north and west, terrorizing the people he meets

February 1540
Coronado sets off in search of the mythical golden cities of Cibola

July 1540
Group dispatched by Coronado discovers the Grand Canyon

May 1541
De Soto crosses the Mississippi River

21 May 1542
De Soto dies and his men return to New Spain (Mexico)

1542
Coronado returns to Mexico City

Conquering Florida

A decade after the disastrous expedition of 1528 (see page 117), Hernando de Soto took over responsibility for conquering Florida for Spain. His expedition took him through Florida and north to the Savannah River before heading west to the Mississippi River. De Soto inflicted great cruelty on the Cherokee, Cree and other native people he met on his travels, but failed to find any gold.

Chasing Cibola

On the western side of North America, another Spaniard went in search of gold, seeking the mythical city of Cibola. Francisco Vásquez de Coronado (c.1510–1554) headed an expedition north through what are now the states of New Mexico, Arizona, Texas and Kansas. His men were the first Europeans to see the Grand Canyon.

The Arizona Desert

Vásquez de Coronado and his expedition crossed through the deserts of New Mexico and Arizona. Here they encountered people such as the Zuni and Hopi, who lived in huts built into the side of the cliffs. The climate was harsh, and many Spaniards lost their lives to Indian attacks.

A Kachina doll – a religious object made by the Hopi of the Arizona Desert.

Hernando de Soto

De Soto (c.1496–1542) was a Spanish nobleman who made his fortune conquering the Inca empire with Pizarro. Now rich, he craved power and in 1537 he was granted the right to conquer and colonize Florida.

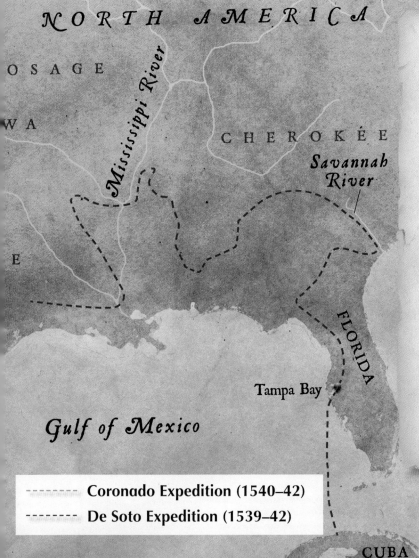

NORTH AMERICA

OSAGE

WA

Mississippi River

CHEROKEE

Savannah River

E

FLORIDA

Tampa Bay

Gulf of Mexico

-------- **Coronado Expedition (1540–42)**

-------- **De Soto Expedition (1539–42)**

CUBA

123

Into Canada

While the Spanish explored Central America and Florida, the French concentrated on what is now Canada. They hoped to find a waterway through North America that would take them to Asia. What they discovered instead became the basis of a vast empire in the Americas.

First steps

In 1534 Jacques Cartier (1491–1557) set out to find a northwest passage to Asia. He sailed into the Gulf of St Lawrence, and returned the following year and discovered the mighty St Lawrence River – the gateway into Canada. Cartier sailed up the river, stopping at Stadacona (modern Québec) and Hochelaga. He named the hill near Hochelaga Mont Réal (Mount Royal), modern-day Montréal.

Woodland around the Great Lakes in full autumn splendour.

Sir Walter Raleigh

English adventurer Walter Raleigh (c.1552–1618) led an expedition in 1585 to set up an English colony in North America. The colony he founded at Roanoke in North Carolina only lasted a year.

It's a Mystery!

In 1587, 100 English settlers under Governor John White arrived on Roanoke Island. White returned to England for supplies, but when he came back in 1590 all the settlers had vanished without trace.

St Lawrence River

Jacques Cartier found it impossible to sail up the St Lawrence River and its tributaries because of the many white-water rapids above Montréal. Samuel de Champlain solved this problem by copying the locals and travelling by canoe.

The Hochelaga negotiated rapids in canoes like this.

French settlers

French fur trappers, traders and fishermen followed Cartier to Canada, but it was not until the next century that an attempt was made to settle the area permanently. Samuel de Champlain (1567–1635) established Québec – one of the first French settlements in Canada. In 1615, he explored Lake Ontario.

Timeline

1534
Cartier explores the coast of Newfoundland

1535–36
Travels up St Lawrence River to Montréal

1587
English colonists settle on Roanoke Island, but have all gone by 1590

1603
De Champlain explores the St Lawrence up to Montréal

1608–09
Founds Québec

1615–16
Rows up Ottawa River by canoe, crosses overland to Lakes Ontario and Oneida

First nations

The French got on well with the native peoples, and used them as guides. De Champlain sided with the Algonquins, Hurons and Montagnais against the Iroquois, who later helped the British throw the French out of Canada.

Chiefs of the Ottawa, who were allies of the French.

The mighty Mississippi

By the late 17th century, Europeans had successfully founded colonies in the south, east and north of North America. But the interior of the continent remained relatively unknown to them. That changed after two extraordinary journeys by French explorers.

The new river

In 1673, fur trader Louis Jolliet (1645–1700), Jesuit priest Jacques Marquette (1637–75) and five others set out from the north to explore a great inland river they had heard about. They canoed down the Wisconsin River into the Mississippi, which they paddled down for more than 1600 km until they met hostile Quapaw people and turned back. The Quapaw had Spanish goods, which suggested that the river emptied into the Gulf of Mexico, where the Spanish had set up colonies.

Cavelier de La Salle

René Robert Cavelier de La Salle (1643–87) was the son of a rich merchant from Rouen in France. He was training to become a priest before choosing a life of adventure and moving to the New World.

This print shows Jolliet and Marquette being paddled down the Mississippi by Illinois allies.

Le Griffon was built with the help of the local Iroquois.

Building Le Griffon

In 1678, La Salle built a ship, *Le Griffon*, at Niagara. It was the first full-size sailing ship on the Great Lakes. He built it to carry the furs he was hoping would pay for his expedition down the river. *Le Griffon* sailed through the Great Lakes and was soon laden with furs, but it sank on its way back to Niagara and the valuable cargo was lost.

What Next?

La Salle claimed the Mississippi basin for France, naming it Louisiana for the king, Louis XIV. This vast territory remained French until 1763. It was sold to the USA in 1803.

Timeline

17 May 1673
Jolliet and Marquette cross Lake Michigan and paddle into Mississippi

17 July 1673
The expedition meets Quapaw people and turns back near the Arkansas River

1678
La Salle sets up headquarters at Niagara on the Great Lakes

21 December 1681
La Salle sets off for the Mississippi

6 April 1682
La Salle reaches the delta; the party splits into three and meets three days later in the Gulf of Mexico

All the way down

In 1681, La Salle set off to explore the Mississippi River. Approaching the Mississippi via the Illinois River, the expedition canoed south until they, too, met the Quapaw near the Arkansas River. This time, the Quapaw allowed the party to continue south. In April 1682, the expedition reached the Mississippi Delta and the sea. The centre of North America was now open to exploration and colonial settlement.

Mississippi Delta

When La Salle's expedition reached the delta at the mouth of the Mississippi, they split up to explore the vast marshes. The city of New Orleans was founded in 1718 to take advantage of the area's natural resources.

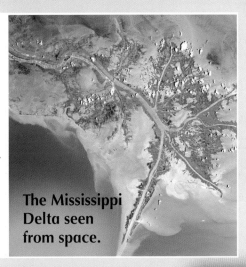

The Mississippi Delta seen from space.

Searching for the Western Sea

The first Spanish, French and English explorers of North America had no idea just how big the continent was. Many believed that there was a sea in the interior that led to the Pacific Ocean. One man set out to find it.

The westward river

Pierre de Charlevoix arrived in Québec in 1720 and departed on his journey the next year. As he paddled through the Great Lakes he asked about the fabled Western Sea. French fur trappers could tell him nothing, while the locals just told him what he wanted to hear. But he did learn of "a great river that flows westwards and empties into the southern sea".

De Charlevoix

Pierre François Xavier de Charlevoix (1682–1761) was a French Jesuit priest of noble birth who first visited the New World in 1705–09. He returned in 1720 to investigate the Western Sea.

De Charlevoix hoped in vain that the Plains Indians such as those depicted in this painting would lead him to the Western Sea.

What Next?

The New Orleans that de Charlevoix visited contained "a hundred shacks". He predicted that one day it would become "an opulent city".

The Missouri River

The Missouri River starts in the Rocky Mountains in southwest Montana. It then flows east and south for 3767 kilometres before joining the Mississippi at St Louis. Its source is close to sources of rivers that flow west into the Columbia River and on into the Pacific Ocean. De Charlevoix guessed correctly that rivers would flow down the west side of the Rockies as well as the east.

The fruitless search

De Charlevoix set off in July 1721, retracing La Salle's route (see page 127) down the Mississippi to New Orleans. He found no Western Sea, as none exists, but became convinced that any westward-flowing river would be found near the headwaters of the Missouri River. This prediction would later be confirmed – but not for another 80 years.

Befriending the Sioux

De Charlevoix guessed that there were people west of the Sioux nation living near the Western Sea. He suggested that the French government should befriend the Sioux. French traders had already formed alliances with them, but a century and a half later, the Sioux would come into bloody conflict with settlers.

Sitting Bull, a 19th-century Sioux chief who fought the US army.

Timeline

23 September 1720
De Charlevoix arrives in Québec and winters there before paddling through the Great Lakes, mapping the shores

29 July 1721
Sets off down the east side of Lake Michigan and into the St Joseph River

September 1721
Stops for a month at Fort St Joseph, where he studies the Miami peoples

December 1721
Spends Christmas at Natchez on the banks of the Mississippi

10 January 1722
Arrives in New Orleans

The new frontier

In 1803 US president Thomas Jefferson bought territory west of the Mississippi River from the French for $15 million. Jefferson commissioned an expedition to find out exactly what it was he had bought.

Heading west

The expedition was led by Jefferson's secretary, Meriwether Lewis, and his friend, William Clark. They were told to explore the newly acquired territory and to find a route through it to the Pacific coast. In May 1804, the pair set off from St Louis on the banks of the Mississippi and canoed up the Missouri River towards the Rocky Mountains.

Timeline

14 May 1804
Lewis and Clark leave St Louis via the Missouri

October 1804
Expedition winters with the Mandan in North Dakota

9 April 1805
Expedition sets off west

September 1805
They cross the Rockies

8 November 1805
They reach the Pacific, building Fort Clatsop to spend the winter

March 1806
Expedition retraces its steps and canoes back down the Missouri

23 September 1806
Expedition returns to St Louis in triumph

Lewis and Clark

Meriwether Lewis (1774–1809), pictured left, and William Clark (1770–1838), right, met while they were serving in the army. In 1803 Lewis asked Clark to become co-leader of the Corps of Discovery, as the expedition was known. The pair worked very well with each other. Lewis was very good at organization, while Clark had vast experience in survival techniques and was a skilled mapmaker. They shared leadership duties, but Clark was the main guide through the dangerous Rockies.

Unlike other Plains Indians, the Mandan lived in permanent villages like this one, where the men are performing a bull dance.

Friendly locals

Lewis and Clark spent their first winter with the Mandan, a friendly tribe of hunters and farmers. While there, they were approached by a Montréal fur trapper, Toussaint Charbonneau, who wished to join the expedition. His wife Sacajawea was a Shoshone Indian. She proved invaluable as an interpreter and helped the expedition through potentially hostile territory.

It's Amazing!

In August 1805 the expedition made first contact with the Shoshone tribe. Their Shoshone guide, Sacajawea, took them to meet the tribe, and recognized its chief as her long-lost brother.

Crossing the Rockies

The expedition rode on horseback through the Rockies. They then paddled down towards the Columbia River. They reached the Pacific coast in November 1805. The route they had found to the Pacific was not easy. During their journey, however, they had made friendly contact with many tribes and found out a lot about this vast territory.

The Rocky Mountains lay across the route to the Pacific Ocean, and proved very difficult to cross.

Hostile territory

The expedition faced many challenges while crossing the Rockies. Grizzly bears constantly attacked them, at one point chasing six men into the river. On another occasion a buffalo charged straight through their camp.

Grizzly bears are a constant threat in the Rockies.

Opening up the west

In the early 1840s, United States territory did not reach as far west as the Pacific Ocean. California was held by Mexico and Oregon was run jointly with Britain. The US government set about settling these regions, hoping eventually to claim them as its own.

What Next?

The first pioneers set out along the newly mapped Oregon Trail in 1843. By 1845 at least 5000 a year were making the journey.

The Oregon Trail

Explorer John Frémont opened up the west to potential settlers. On his first expedition in 1842, he surveyed the route from the Mississippi west to the South Pass – a 32-km-wide passage through the Rockies. The next year, he carried on through the pass and opened up the Oregon Trail to the Columbia River and the coast.

Pioneers on the Oregon Trail travelled in trains of about 10 wagons.

Frémont carried this flag on all his expeditions. The eagle is holding a pipe as a sign of friendship to the Indians.

Carrying the flag

John Frémont (1813–90) was the son of a French school teacher. From 1838 he surveyed new territories for the US Army Topographical Corps. He subsequently made a fortune during the California Gold Rush of 1848, but lost all his money and died in poverty.

Kit Carson

Kit Carson (1809–68) was a fur trapper from Boone's Lick, Missouri, hired by Frémont as a guide to the Rocky Mountains. Frémont described Carson as the finest mountain man he had ever met. Carson worked with Frémont on all his expeditions.

The California Trail

In 1845, Frémont set out again, and opened up a trail via the Great Salt Lake to Sacramento in California. After a war with Mexico, California and other Mexican areas were taken by the US by 1847. By then, the British had already given up all claims on Oregon. The territory of the USA now reached the Pacific coast, and new settlers began to travel there along the routes pioneered by Frémont.

Timeline

1842
Frémont surveys a route from the Mississippi to the South Pass

1843–44
On his second journey, Frémont opens up the Oregon Trail then travels to southern California and treks east through Sierra Nevada

March 1845
Frémont surveys California Trail to Sacramento

March 1846
Frémont raises US flag in California

1848
Treaty of Guadalupe–Hidalgo gives US control of California, Nevada, Utah, and parts of Arizona and New Mexico

The Great Salt Lake

On 6 September 1843, Frémont and his team saw the Great Salt Lake, describing the area as suitable for settlement. This attracted Brigham Young's Christian sect, the Mormons, to the area, although Young later described it as a desert.

The water in the Great Salt Lake is even saltier than sea water.

Scientific explorers

After explorers had discovered new lands, scientists set out to find out about these lands' strange new plants and wildlife. Their discoveries, most notably in the rich environment of the Amazon rainforest, have led to great advances in scientific knowledge.

South American studies

French scientist Charles-Marie de la Condamine (1701–74) sailed to Ecuador in 1735. He wanted to measure the size and shape of the world – a science known as geodesy. He stayed to study the area's plants and animals. In the early 1800s German Alexander von Humboldt and Frenchman Aimé Bonpland (1773–1858) explored the Andes, recording 3000 new plant species.

Alexander von Humboldt

Humboldt (1769–1859) explored the Orinoco River in Venezuela, and then travelled down the Andes from the Caribbean to Peru. He made important discoveries in many scientific fields and was described by Charles Darwin as "the greatest scientific traveller who ever lived".

Drawings by Bates of some of the butterflies he found in Amazonia.

The collector

Henry Bates (1825–92) was an English clerk with an avid interest in botany. After 11 years in South America, he returned to Britain with about 14,000 insect and butterfly specimens. At least half of them were unknown to European scientists of the time.

The great age

The 19th century was the great age of scientific exploration. Henry Bates, Alfred Wallace (1823–1913) and Richard Spruce (1817–93) all spent years in the Amazon, collecting animal and plant specimens. Charles Darwin (1809–82) visited the offshore Galápagos Islands in 1835. His observations of the islands' extraordinary wildlife led him to develop his ideas about how species develop into the theory of evolution.

The Amazon rainforest, one of the richest natural environments in the world, where thousands or even millions of species are yet to be discovered.

What Next?

After four years in the Amazon rainforest, Alfred Wallace set sail for home in 1852. Sadly, his ship caught fire off Bermuda and he lost all his specimens and notes.

Modern discoveries

Scientists are discovering more species of animal and plant than ever. Nearly 2 million have been described, but there may be as many as 50 million left to discover. In the last 20 years alone, nearly 2000 new species of amphibian have been found.

New species of amphibian, such as this South American treefrog, are discovered every year.

Timeline

1735–44
La Condamine studies wildlife in Ecuador

1799–1804
Humboldt and Bonpland explore the River Orinoco and the Andes

1832–35
Darwin sails around South America and the Galápagos Islands on board the *Beagle*

1848–52
Wallace collects thousands of specimens but loses them to a fire

1849–64
Spruce collects plant specimens in Amazonia

1850–59
Bates collects insect specimens in Amazonia

Darwin in the Galápagos

Charles Darwin studied medicine and then for the priesthood, giving up on both ideas. With nothing else to do he took the post of naturalist on board the Beagle, a survey ship bound for South America. This is an extract from his account of his visit to the Galápagos Islands off the coast of Chile – a visit that was to inform his revolutionary theory of the evolution of the species.

The different finches of the islands have beaks of many shapes and sizes, depending on their feeding habits.

17 September 1835

The Bay swarmed with animals. Fish, sharks and turtles popped their heads up all around. These islands are paradises for all sorts of reptiles. There are three kinds of turtle, and there are so many tortoises that a single ship's company caught over 500 in a very short time. The little birds are very trusting, and hopped about within three or four feet of us.

21 September

In my walk I met two very large tortoises (circumference of shell about 7 feet). One ate a cactus and then quietly walked away. The other gave a deep and loud hiss and drew back his head. They were so heavy I could barely lift them off the ground. Surrounded by the black lava, the leafless shrubs and large cacti, they look like old-fashioned, ancient animals; or rather inhabitants of some other planet.

Galápagos Islands

Santiago
Baltra
Rabida
Fernandina
Santa Fe
San Cristobal
Isabela
Santa Cruz
Floreana
Española

25 September

Mr Lawson remembers seeing a terrapin which six men could scarcely lift and two could not turn over on its back. These immense creatures must be very old. In the year 1830, one was caught by whalers. It had various dates carved on its shell, and one was 1786. The only reason it was not carried away there and then must have been that it was too big for two men to manage. The whalers always send off their men in pairs to hunt.

27 September

I collected all the animals, plants, insects and reptiles from this island. I will compare these specimens with creatures from elsewhere. In this way, I shall work out to which district or centre of creation the organized beings of these islands must be attached.

THE PACIFIC AND AUSTRALIA

Although European explorers had crossed the Pacific Ocean by the 16th century, most of this vast body of water was still known only to Polynesian travellers. Europeans believed that the Pacific bordered a vast southern continent, but nobody was sure where it was. Expeditions set sail to discover this 'new' continent. During their travels, European navigators mapped the ocean, explored its islands and found a smaller continent.

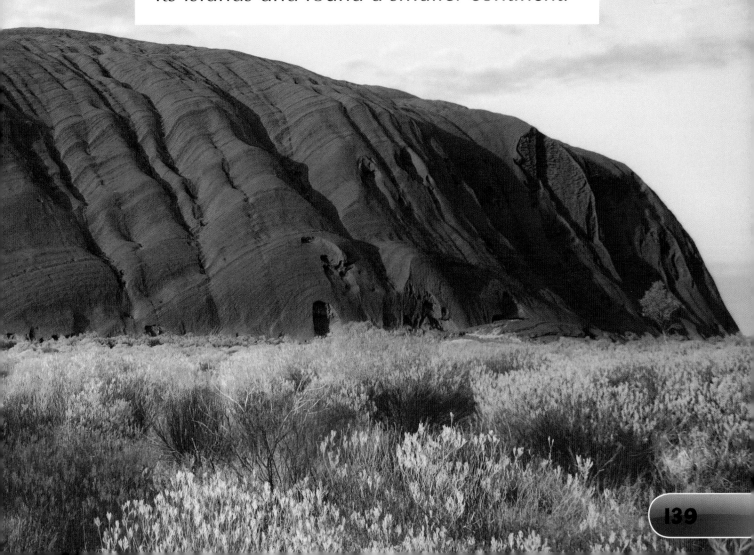

The incredible Polynesians

Long before Europeans arrived in the Pacific Ocean, navigators had already explored the ocean and colonized its many islands. Their perilous voyages are among the most remarkable human expeditions of all time.

Who were they?

The first inhabitants of the Pacific islands moved east from Indonesia in about 2000 BC, reaching Fiji, Tonga and Samoa by 1000 BC. Here they developed a distinctive Polynesian culture. In about 200 BC they began to seek new islands, sailing east to Tahiti and Easter Island, north to Hawaii, then eventually south to Aotearoa (New Zealand).

A Polynesian double canoe, similar in design to a modern-day catamaran.

The Maori

Aotearoa was the last island group to be colonized. The Maori, as the new settlers were known, adapted their customs to live off the islands' unique animals and plants.

It's Amazing!

When Captain Cook measured a Maori canoe in Aotearoa in 1770, he found it was longer than the ship he was sailing.

A Maori man with traditional facial tattoos.

Timeline

More than 800 of these giant statues stand on Easter Island. Nobody knows why they were made.

Easter Island

Easter Island is more than 1600 km from its nearest island neighbour, and is so remote that the islanders believed they were the only people on Earth. They were the only Polynesians to develop a form of writing.

Navigation techniques

The Polynesians had no instruments to guide them. Instead, they navigated by observing changes in the wind and currents, looking at wave patterns and following migrating birds. They also used the sun and stars: each island had its 'on top' star, so that when, for example, Sirius was overhead, they knew they were in the same latitude as Tahiti. Using these simple methods, they colonized the entire Pacific Ocean.

Stick charts

Polynesian navigators were trained using a stick chart, such as this one from the Marshall Islands. The charts were made of a network of palm sticks tied together with coconut fibre. Shells threaded on to the sticks marked the position of each island relative to the ocean currents, allowing a navigator to learn the geography of the region.

Into the southern seas

In the 16th century, following Magellan's lead, a number of Spanish and Portuguese explorers set out across the Pacific, discovering new islands and attempting to colonize the region with European settlers.

Solomon Islands

Mendaña explored many of the Solomon Islands. Conflict broke out with the inhabitants when the Spanish went in search of food.

A mask (right) and paddle (above) from the Solomon Islands.

Failed settlers

In 1567, Alvaro de Mendaña (1541–95) sailed west from Peru, intending to convert people to Christianity and set up a Spanish settlement. He discovered the Solomon Islands, but it was a disastrous voyage. His ship was almost destroyed in a hurricane, forcing the crew to make sails out of blankets. Most of the crew died before they could reach safety. Almost 30 years later, Mendaña died in a failed attempt to settle the Solomons.

Another try

In 1605, Pedro Fernández de Quirós (1565–1614) set out to discover the southern continent. He visited the Cook Islands and Vanuatu, but then abandoned the expedition. Luis Váez de Torres (c.1565–1613) took over the expedition and sailed round New Guinea.

Forgotten lands

After Mendaña left the Solomons in 1568, the islands were completely forgotten until 1767, while Torres's voyage around New Guinea in 1607 was not properly recognised until 1762.

Fishermen on the Solomon islands.

Men from New Guinea perform a ceremonial dance.

It's Amazing!

Ancient Greek philosopher Ptolemy thought that most of the Earth was covered by land, so there must be a vast continent in the far south. This was widely believed right up to the 18th century.

Timeline

February 1568
Mendaña discovers Solomon Islands

15 August 1568
Two ships sail for home but are separated; Mendaña lands in America in November

April 1595
Sets out again for the Solomons, but dies in the Santa Cruz islands

21 December 1605
Quirós searches for the southern continent

May 1606
Quirós reaches Vanuatu then sails for home; Torres takes over

May 1607
Torres sails between New Guinea and Australia

Round Australia

In two epic voyages, the Dutch explorer Abel Tasman sailed round Australia and explored its northern coast. Despite proving that this new continent was not part of a larger southern continent, his expeditions were considered a failure.

What Next?
The Dutch never publicized Tasman's voyages, as they did not want anyone else to know about the newly discovered lands in the Pacific.

New Guinea

Batavia

→ **First expedition (1642–43)**

← **Second expedition (1644)**

Torres Strait

Pacific Ocean

Australia

Abel Tasman

Abel Tasman (1603–59) was born in Lutjegast, Holland. In 1634, he moved to Batavia (now Jakarta) on Java, where he was employed as a captain by the Dutch East India Company. After his voyages, he became a judge in Batavia.

Van Diemen's Land

South of the continent

In 1642, Tasman sailed west from Batavia across the Indian Ocean to Mauritius. His mission was to explore the land south of Java and find a passage between the Indian and Pacific oceans to lead Dutch sailors to the riches of South America. From Mauritius, Tasman sailed south and east, becoming the first European to visit Tasmania (which he named Van Diemen's Land), New Zealand and Fiji. The voyage took him all the way round Australia, and proved conclusively that it was not the fabled "Great South Land".

Exploration

For his second voyage, Tasman attempted to establish the relationships of New Guinea, Australia, the new Van Diemen's Land, and the "unknown South Land" (Antarctica). However, he failed to recognize the Torres Strait, and returned to Batavia after sailing along Australia's north coast.

Tasman Sea

New Zealand

Timeline

14 August 1642
Tasman sets sail from Batavia to find a short cut to Chile and explore the "Great South Land"

13 December 1642
Sights South Island of New Zealand, which he believes to be part of the southern continent; mistakes strait between the islands for a bay

April 1643
Discovers Fiji

29 February 1644
Sets sail for New Guinea and Australia via the Torres Strait, which he mistakes for a bay; explores north coast of Australia then returns to Batavia

Dutch East Indies

The Dutch East India Company was set up in 1602 to challenge Spanish and Portuguese control of the spice trade. Basing itself in Batavia, its large fleet of ships quickly gained control of many of the seas around southeast Asia.

A 17th-century painting of the Dutch East India Company's private fleet.

The first voyage of Captain Cook

Despite many voyages across the Pacific, the ocean remained largely unknown to Europeans well into the 18th century. So the quest for the great southern continent remained as intense as ever.

Circling New Zealand

In 1768, the Royal Society, a body set up in the UK to promote science, asked James Cook to supervise an expedition to Tahiti. They wanted him to observe the path of the planet Venus across the sun. The British Admiralty supported the expedition, hoping to discover the great southern continent. Cook arrived in the south Pacific in April 1769 and sailed right round both islands of New Zealand, proving they were not part of a larger continent.

Timeline

26 August 1768
Cook leaves Plymouth; collects plant specimens on Tierra del Fuego

13 April 1769
Anchors off Tahiti for three months

October 1769
Reaches New Zealand and sails around the two islands

29 April 1770
Lands at Botany Bay

October 1770
Sails up west coast of Australia, round northern tip and reaches Batavia via the Torres Strait

Captain James Cook

James Cook (1728–79) was born in Yorkshire, England, the son of a poor farmer. He first went to sea aged 14 to work on a coal ship. He joined the Royal Navy in 1755, and quickly worked his way up through the ranks. His navigational skills and experience of observing eclipses made him the ideal person to lead the three missions to the South Seas.

The *Endeavour*

The *Endeavour* was a converted coal ship similar to the ones Cook sailed in when he first went to sea. The ship was not elegant or fast but it was large. It was roomy enough to accommodate a crew of 94 men plus their stores, and tough enough for the long voyage.

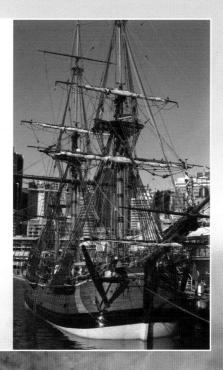

A replica of the *Endeavour* in Whitby, Yorkshire.

First landing

Cook sailed west across the Tasman Sea, sighting land on the southeast coast of Australia at Point Hicks on 19 April. Ten days later he landed at Botany Bay. Continuing northwards, Cook ran aground on the Great Barrier Reef and was forced to land to make repairs. He then sailed to Batavia via the Torres Strait before returning home.

Cook's crew were the first Europeans to see kangaroos like this one.

It's Amazing!

When Cook's crew first saw a kangaroo, they were unsure what sort of animal it was. The size of a deer, but jumping like a hare, they decided it must be a "kind of stag".

New discoveries

Naturalists Joseph Banks and Daniel Solander were on board the *Endeavour*, along with painter Sydney Parkinson. Together, they recorded many new exotic plants, animals and insects.

A drawing by Sydney Parkinson of Red Honeysuckle.

147

Discovering Antarctica

For his second expedition, Cook was sent on a final search for the legendary southern continent. The British Admiralty was still not sure whether the southern continent really existed.

Crossing the Circle

Cook sailed south down the Atlantic Ocean and continued south until he crossed the Antarctic Circle – the first explorer to do so. He then sailed through the Southern Ocean to New Zealand and took on more supplies before heading south again. The mythical continent was thought to lie somewhere between New Zealand and Cape Horn.

What next?

After his second voyage, Cook wrote a report on how to prevent scurvy – a potentially fatal disease caused by a lack of vitamin C.

Timeline

13 July 1772
Cook sets sail with two ships in search of the southern continent

17 January 1773
Crosses Antarctic Circle and sails to New Zealand for supplies

November 1774
Sailing south to Antarctica, Cook's two ships are separated; the *Adventure* returns to England

December 1774
The *Resolution* is surrounded by icebergs

29 July 1775
Having survived the winter, Cook returns home via Cape Horn

A drawing from 1809 of the *Resolution* surrounded by pack ice off Antarctica.

The *Resolution*

Cook made his second voyage with the *Resolution* and the *Adventure*. They were both converted coal ships, whose strong hulls protected them against icebergs. The *Resolution* was originally named the *Drake,* after explorer and pirate Sir Francis Drake, but this was changed for fear of upsetting the Spanish.

Cook attends a village meeting on Tahiti.

Tahiti

On each of his voyages, Cook stopped off in Tahiti. When he saw that Tahitians and Easter Islanders could understand each other, he began to suspect that South Sea islanders all shared a common ancestry.

The southern continent

Finding only a few small islands, Cook returned to New Zealand before sailing south again. He crossed the Antarctic Circle twice more before icebergs forced him north. Having sailed right round the South Pole, he could rule out the existence of a massive continent. However, he believed that he had found a large piece of land near the Pole.

The coastline of Antarctica, which Cook believed he saw.

Sea chronometer

Until Cook's time, navigators had been able to calculate latitude (position north–south) but not longitude (east–west). In 1760, James Harrison developed the chronometer for accurately measuring longitude. Cook used this on his second voyage.

The H5, one of Harrison's chronometers.

Cook's final voyage

On his final voyage, Cook set out to find the northwest passage between the Atlantic and Pacific oceans. Two other expeditions searched for a passage from the Atlantic side, while Cook looked for one from the Pacific.

Finding Hawaii

Setting sail with both the *Resolution* and the *Discovery*, Cook left England in July 1776. He sailed south to Cape Town and then across the Indian Ocean to New Zealand. He re-visited Tahiti, and what are now known as the Cook Islands. He then sailed north, finding the previously unknown volcanic Hawaiian Islands, which he named the Sandwich Isles.

It's Amazing!

Among the crew of the *Resolution* was William Bligh. Years later, in 1787, he was made captain of HMS *Bounty*. His crew mutinied and set Bligh and 18 others adrift in a small boat.

The NuuChahNulth

As Cook sailed up the American coast, he missed the strait between Vancouver Island and the mainland, and anchored in Nootka Sound. Here, the local NuuChahNulth people greeted him wearing elaborate masks and painted faces.

A NuuChahNulth totem pole carved from a cedar tree.

Timeline

12 July 1776
Cook sets sail from Plymouth

January 1777
Heads to New Zealand and on to Tahiti and the Cook Islands

December 1777
Lands on an island he calls Christmas Island

January 1778
Reaches Hawaii, then cruises up the North American coastline

18 August 1778
Becomes icebound in the Arctic Ocean and heads south again

17 January 1779
Returns to Hawaii

14 February 1779
Cook is killed on Hawaii Island

The Aleutian Islands

The Aleutian Islands stretch from southwest Alaska along the south of the Bering Sea. Vitus Bering was the first to explore the islands in 1741 (see pages 50–51). Cook sailed along the eastern end of the chain before he headed north into the Bering Sea.

Cook's final days

In spring and summer 1778, Cook explored the North American coast from Oregon north to Alaska. He sailed down the Aleutian Islands before turning north again into the Bering Sea. He became increasingly unsure that he would find the passage. When ice surrounded his ships, he headed back to Hawaii, where he was killed on 14 February 1779.

Mauna Kea – the largest of five volcanoes on Hawaii Island.

The Death of Cook

Cook tried to deal fairly with the people he met. In Hawaii, however, the islanders stole one of his small boats. Cook planned to take the local king hostage to get his boat back. As Cook negotiated, his crew opened fire and the islanders stabbed Cook to death.

Knives are drawn as Cook's men open fire.

Cook lands in Australia

Captain James Cook first caught sight of the southeast tip of Australia on 19 April 1770. He then sailed Endeavour northeast up the coast. Sailing with him were Tupia, a native of Tahiti, and two naturalists, Joseph Banks and Daniel Solander. This is his account of landing at Botany Bay.

Saturday 28 April

We are now less than two miles from the shore, so Mr Banks, Dr Solander, Tupia and I set off towards land in a small boat. Four or five natives took to the woods as we approached the shore. To our disappointment, we could find no safe place to land.

In the morning, we found a bay that was quite well sheltered from the wind. I decided to sail the ship into this bay, and sent the master ahead to see how we could enter it.

Sunday 29 April

As we sailed by, we saw several natives on both sides of the bay. There were a few huts, men, women and children on the south shore, and I approached by rowing boat hoping to speak with them. As we came near, they all took off, except two men who seemed resolved to oppose our landing. When I saw this, I immediately ordered the oarsmen to stop rowing so that I could speak to the two men. But neither Tupia nor any other of my men could understand one word they said. Shortly after this we landed, and as soon as we did so, they threw two darts at us.

Sunday 6 May

In the evening, the small sailing yawl returned from a fishing expedition. They caught two stingrays weighing near 600 pounds. I have given this place the name of Botany Bay, in honour of the great quantity of new plants that Mr Banks and Dr Solander have collected here.

The tragic voyage of La Pérouse

Captain Cook's voyages did much to map the Pacific Ocean and clear up any confusion about the southern continent. But the French government wanted to know more. In 1785 they sent a naval expedition to the ocean, led by Comte de La Pérouse.

The mission

La Pérouse's mission was to fill any gaps in the knowledge of the Pacific Ocean left by Cook. La Pérouse set sail from France with two ships. After rounding Cape Horn, he cruised up the eastern Pacific to Alaska, but failed to find any northwest passage. He then headed across the ocean to China.

NORTH AMERICA

ALASKA

KAMCHATKA

Petropavlovsk

ASIA

CALIFORNIA

MACAU

PHILIPPINES

Pacific Ocean

SANTA CRUZ ISLANDS

AUSTRALIA

EASTER ISLAND

Botany Bay

N

NW

NE

E

It's a Mystery!

In 1828 it was discovered that La Pérouse's ships had run aground in the Santa Cruz Islands. The islanders had killed some of the crew, while others had built a small boat to sail to safety. What happened to them after that has never been discovered.

Timeline

1 August 1785
La Pérouse leaves France with the *Boussole* and the *Astrolabe*

April 1786
Enters the Pacific and heads north

24 September 1786
Leaves California and sails west

September 1787
Reaches Petropavlovsk in Kamchatka, where he receives orders to sail to Australia

24 January 1788
Sails into Botany Bay

10 March 1788
Sails north and is never seen again

1828
French explorers find wrecks of the two ships on Santa Cruz Islands

Comte de La Pérouse

Jean-François de Galaup, Comte (Count) de La Pérouse (1741–88), was a French nobleman who joined the navy aged 15. By the early 1780s he had commanded a number of ships, making him the ideal candidate for the expedition of 1785.

EUROPE

FRANCE

AFRICA

SOUTH AMERICA

Valparaiso

Cape Horn

Lost at sea

La Pérouse sailed north to the Kamchatka Peninsula in Siberia, where a letter from France ordered him to investigate a settlement in New South Wales, Australia. He reached Botany Bay just after the British had set up a prison colony there. He headed north again towards New Guinea, but neither he nor his crew were ever seen again.

La Pérouse's legacy

From the various places he landed, La Pérouse took the opportunity to send back to Europe the logs, papers, paintings and charts made during his voyage. These were published in an atlas in 1798.

A painting of Easter Island from La Pérouse's atlas.

Inland Australia

In 1788, the first British settlers arrived in Sydney Cove to set up a prison colony there. The coast of Australia was still little known and the vast interior totally unexplored.

Opening up the continent

From 1798–99, the English naval captain Matthew Flinders (1774–1814) and the surgeon George Bass (1771–1803) mapped much of the coastline south of Sydney. They also sailed around Tasmania, proving it was an island. Two years later, Flinders circled the whole continent. The interior of Australia remained a mystery until 1813, when a route was discovered through the Blue Mountains that lay behind Sydney.

Charles Sturt

Charles Sturt (1795–1869) was born in India the son of a British judge. He was educated in England before going to Australia in 1826 as a soldier to guard convicts. He liked the country immediately and became one of its first inland explorers.

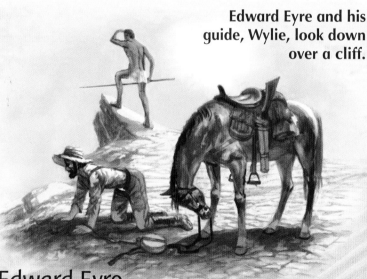

Edward Eyre and his guide, Wylie, look down over a cliff.

Edward Eyre

Englishman Edward Eyre (1815–1901) emigrated to Australia aged 17. He became the manager of a sheep station in South Australia, and explored the region in 1839. A year later, he set off across southern Australia in search of land for grazing.

It's Amazing!

Before 1824, the name 'Australia' applied to the whole South Pacific region. The continent we know by this name today was called Terra Australis or New Holland.

Australian Aborigines

The aboriginal people walked across a land bridge (no longer there) from Asia to Australia about 40,000 years ago and slowly spread across the continent. They were nomadic hunters and gatherers who lived in small groups. Each group spoke its own language and had its own laws.

This boy is holding two boomerangs – Aboriginal tools for hunting.

The Simpson Desert in the centre of Australia, visited by Charles Sturt in 1845.

Timeline

1788
First convicts and guards arrive at Sydney Cove

1798–99
Matthew Flinders and George Bass map the southwest coast

1801–03
Flinders sails round Australia

1829–30
Charles Sturt discovers the River Darling

1839–40
Edward Eyre explores inland South Australia

1841
Eyre crosses from Adelaide to Western Australia

1844–46
Sturt treks inland to the Simpson Desert

Into the interior

In two expeditions in 1828 and 1830, Charles Sturt mapped Australia's two major rivers, the Murray and Darling. This opened up what is now inland New South Wales to farmers and settlers. Sturt later ventured towards the centre of Australia looking for an inland sea, but only found desert. In 1841 Edward Eyre trekked from Adelaide in South Australia west along the arid coast of the Great Australian Bight to Albany at the southern tip of Western Australia. With not a single river along the route, Eyre was forced to dig deep wells in the sand, and would have died if it hadn't started to rain.

So close, yet so far!

Many people believed Australia was so vast it must contain an inland sea. In 1860, the South Australian government decided to find out. It offered a large cash prize to the first person to cross the continent from south to north.

Early setbacks

Robert Burke's expedition seemed well equipped. It set out from Melbourne with 18 men, 24 camels, 28 horses and 21 tonnes of provisions. But when the camel master and the doctor quit at Menindee, 640 km north of Melbourne, Burke decided to leave most of his supplies behind and continue with a small group. At Cooper's Creek, he left William Brahe in charge of the remaining party, and set out north with William Wills, John King, Charles Gray and provisions for 12 weeks.

The mudflats at the Gulf of Carpentaria.

Timeline

21 August 1860
Burke's expedition sets out from Melbourne

19 October 1860
Two men drop out at Menindee

16 December 1860
Burke establishes supply depot at Cooper's Creek

9 February 1861
Expedition reaches the tidal Flinders River but does not see the sea

21 April 1861
Burke, Wills and King return to find Cooper's Creek deserted

June 1861
Burke and Wills die of starvation; King is rescued by Aborigines

Burke and Wills

Robert O'Hara Burke (1821–61), left, was born in Ireland and emigrated to Australia, where he became a police officer in Melbourne. His expedition into the interior was his first experience of the Australian outback (remote dry areas). William John Wills (1834–61), right, became Burke's second-in-command when the camel master defected.

Beasts of burden

Camels are not native to Australia, but were introduced in the 1840s to carry goods through the outback. Some of them escaped, and were the ancestors of Australia's wild camel population.

Almost there

On 9 February 1861, Burke's party reached the tidal estuary of the Flinders River in the Gulf of Carpentaria. They never saw the coast because wide mudflats stood between them and the sea. Almost immediately they headed south again, with Gray dying of dysentery on the way. In April, they arrived at Cooper's Creek to find it deserted. Within two months, Burke and Wills had both died of starvation.

What Next?

Robert Burke was criticized for his poor handling of the expedition, but both he and Wills were later recognized for their bravery by a memorial in Melbourne.

Lost in the bush

When Burke and his two colleagues arrived back in Cooper's Creek, William Brahe had left just hours earlier. Wills and King wanted to try to catch him up, but Burke insisted on heading for Mount Hopeless 240 km to the southwest. Their food ran out, and Burke and Wills died. King was rescued when he was found by Aborigines.

Burke, Wills and King were lost in the bush. Only King survived.

McDouall Stuart

Scottish-born John McDouall Stuart (1815–66) moved to South Australia in 1838 to work as a surveyor. In 1844, he joined Charles Sturt's unsuccessful expedition to reach the centre of the continent (see pages 156–157).

Winning the prize

The prize offered by the South Australian government to cross the continent from south to north proved irresistible to John Stuart. He was so determined to win he made three attempts in just two years!

Failed expedition

In March 1860, Stuart set out from Adelaide in South Australia with just two travel companions. A month later, he made it just over half way there, reaching Tenant Creek. Here, he had to turn back because Aborigines had set fire to the bush in front of him to defend their land.

The view from the summit of Central Mount Stuart.

The British flag is raised in triumph on the shores of the Indian Ocean.

Mount Stuart

On his first attempt to cross Australia, Stuart reached the dead centre of the continent. He named a nearby hill Central Mount Sturt "after the father of Australian exploration". The hill was later renamed Central Mount Stuart after its discoverer.

Pride of Adelaide

The city of Adelaide was founded in 1836, when the British established a colony in South Australia. The city was anxious to make its mark on Australian history, so it offered the prize to cross the continent in 1860.

A statue of John McDouall Stuart in Adelaide.

Try and try again

On his second attempt in early 1861, with a far larger party of 13 men and 49 horses, Stuart came within 320 km of the sea, but turned back when a thicket of thorn bushes blocked his way. In October 1861, he tried again. This time he reached the north coast of Australia at Chambers Bay. The continent had been successfully crossed at last.

Timeline

2 March 1860
Stuart and two companions leave Adelaide to cross Australia, but turn back half way

1 January 1861
Stuart sets off again

September 1861
Returns to Adelaide after getting within 320 km of the north coast

October 1861
Begins third attempt to cross Australia

July 1862
Reaches Indian Ocean

December 1862
Returns home having lost the use of his limbs due to scurvy

What Next?

An overland telegraph line was opened along Stuart's route nine years later. From Darwin on the north coast, the line ran under the sea, connecting Australia to Indonesia and Asia.

A raft of discovery

Most explorers left home in search of adventure or wealth, or to discover new lands to settle. Very few set out to prove a personal theory that could revolutionize history. Thor Heyerdahl was one such explorer.

Thor Heyerdahl

Norwegian explorer Thor Heyerdahl (1914–2002) became fascinated by Polynesia while at university. He lived for a year with his wife in the wild in Tahiti, but found the experience difficult to cope with.

The new theory

The accepted view about the origins of the Polynesians is that their ancestors populated the Pacific islands from southeast Asia by around AD 1000 (see pages 140–141). However, Thor Heyerdahl was convinced that the Pacific islands had been colonized in two big migrations from the Americas in the east, the first by AD 500, and the second in about AD 1100.

Kon-Tiki – a raft just 13.7 m long and 5.5 m wide.

Inca rafts

The Spanish forces who conquered the Inca Empire (see pages 120–121) made drawings of Inca rafts built to sail on Lake Titicaca. These formed the basis of *Kon-Tiki*'s design.

People around Lake Titicaca still make boats out of reeds, similar to the boats of the Incas.

A raft across the Pacific

Heyerdahl set out to prove his theory by building a balsawood and bamboo raft similar to those of the Incas. Named *Kon-Tiki* after a Polynesian god, the raft set out from Peru on a 101-day journey that took Heyerdahl and his crew 8000 km across the Pacific to Raroia in the Tuamotu Islands in Tahiti. Heyerdahl had shown that the first Polynesians could indeed have sailed from South America. However, there is no proof that they made such a journey.

Sweet potato

Most historians believe that early Polynesians probably sailed as far east as South America, as both the Maoris of New Zealand and the Polynesians of the eastern Pacific had cultivated the sweet potato, a native plant of that continent. Heyerdahl claimed that native South Americans had taken the sweet potato with them on their rafts across the Pacific.

Timeline

28 April 1947
Thor Heyerdahl and his crew of five on board *Kon-Tiki* leave Peru and are carried across the eastern Pacific by the prevailing winds

May–July 1947
During the expedition, the crew survive as the early navigators would have done

7 August 1947
Kon-Tiki hits a reef at Raroia in the Tuamotu Islands

1970
Heyerdahl sails *Ra II* across the Atlantic

1978
Sails the *Tigris* from Iraq to Pakistan

What Next?

In 1969, Heyerdahl sailed Ra II, a reed boat across the Atlantic. In 1978, he sailed another reed boat, the Tigris, from Iraq to Pakistan, and then to Djibouti.

INTO AFRICA

By the early 1500s, the Portuguese had explored most of the African coastline, but the interior of the continent remained unknown to Europeans. They knew nothing of its great empires and kingdoms, and even less about its great rivers – the Nile, Niger, Congo and Zambezi. In the late 18th century, European explorers set out to explore this great, unknown continent.

The course of the Niger

In 1788 Joseph Banks, who had sailed with Captain Cook on his first voyage to the Pacific, founded the Africa Association in London. One of the association's first acts was to commission Mungo Park to explore the Niger – the great river that ran through west Africa.

First sight of the river

Park arrived at the mouth of the River Gambia in 1795 and headed inland. He caught a fever, delaying the expedition for two months. He was then forced to travel with only two guides, as most local people refused to accompany him. Park was thus easy prey for the Muslim soldiers who captured him near the Senegal River and held him captive for five months. He escaped and made his way to Ségou on the banks of the Niger.

Mungo Park

Scot Mungo Park (1771–1806) was a medical officer for the East India Company. Joseph Banks asked Park to explore the Niger because he was impressed by his fine descriptions of new species of fish.

It's Amazing!

When he fell gravely ill, Park was nursed back to health by the inhabitants of a small village on the banks of the Niger.

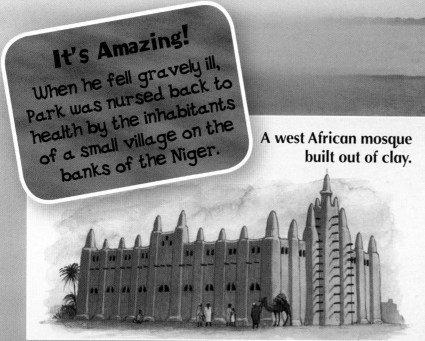

A west African mosque built out of clay.

Muslim lands

The River Niger flowed through the heartland of Muslim west Africa. The great Muslim Mali Empire had ruled the area from the 13th to the 17th centuries, and Timbuktu to the north of the river had been a major Islamic cultural centre. Christians such as Park were unwelcome visitors.

River Niger

The Niger rises in the highlands of Guinea and flows northeast to Timbuktu in Mali before turning to empty into the Gulf of Guinea. Early European explorers were puzzled by the way it flowed away from the coast.

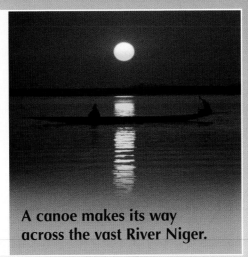

A canoe makes its way across the vast River Niger.

Timeline

July 1795
Park heads inland from mouth of the Gambia

February 1796
Park is captured by Arab soldiers

June 1796
Escapes and reaches Ségou on the Niger

April 1805
Park sets off on second expedition

August 1805
Sails down the Niger past Timbuktu

1806
At the Bussa Falls, Park is attacked and drowns in the river

Death at the Falls

Back home, Park's account of his journey, *Travels in the Interior Districts of Africa*, brought him great fame. In 1805, he returned to follow the Niger along its entire length. He followed the river past Timbuktu, where it bends south. He paddled down to the Bussa Falls in present-day northern Nigeria. Here he was attacked by hostile locals, fell into the rapids and drowned.

Mali women stride along the banks of the River Niger.

The Niger's end

Despite Park's two expeditions, the exact course of the Niger remained unknown, so a new expedition was organized. In 1822, British explorers Dixon Denham, Hugh Clapperton and Walter Oudney set out from Tripoli, North Africa, to see if the river passed through the powerful sultanate (Muslim kingdom) of Kanem-Bornu around Lake Chad.

Hugh Clapperton

At age 17, Scottish-born Clapperton (1788–1827) left home to join the navy. He had become a lieutenant by the time he was asked to join the expedition to the Niger. He was much praised for his opposition to slave trading in the region.

Sahara Desert

Tripoli

Muzug

- - - - **Oudney/Clapperton journey 1822–25**
- - - - **Clapperton/Lander journey 1825–27**
- - - - **Lander brothers' journey 1830**
✝ **Place of death**

Timbuktu

River Niger

Katsina

Sokoto   *Kano*   *Lake Chad*

Yauri

✝ Clapperton 1827

✝ Oudney 1824

Kukawa

Bussa

River Benue

Badagri

Atlantic Ocean

Gulf of Guinea   *Brass*   ✝ Lander 1834

Fernando Po

NW

W

Across the Sahara

After several arguments, Denham separated from the other two, leaving Clapperton and Oudney to become the first Europeans to see Lake Chad. The pair then set out to trace the Niger's path, but Oudney fell ill and died. Clapperton met up with Denham and they returned to England.

Timeline

February 1822
Clapperton, Oudney and Denham set off from Tripoli

February 1823
Clapperton and Oudney see Lake Chad

December 1825
Clapperton and Lander cross the Niger at Bussa

April 1827
Clapperton dies of dysentery

January 1830
Lander brothers set off for the Niger

November 1830
Landers are captured by Igbo and sold to a slave trader; Richard finishes his voyage paddling a royal canoe

The Igbo

As the Landers paddled down the Niger (see below), they were captured and held for ransom by the Igbo king. A slave trader bought the brothers and held John in captivity for a time. Richard worked as a slave on the 40-paddle royal canoe. It was on this canoe that Richard Lander completed the journey to the mouth of the Niger.

An elaborate ceremonial Igbo mask.

Into the sea

Accompanied by his servant, Richard Lemon Lander (1804–34), Clapperton returned to the Niger in 1825. He headed north from the Gulf of Guinea and travelled in a roundabout route to Sokoto. Here Clapperton died, and Lander headed back to London. Lander returned in 1830 with his brother John (1807–39). Heading inland from Badagri, they reached the Niger upstream from Bussa and then paddled down the river. Richard made it to the estuary, proving that the Niger flowed into the Gulf of Guinea.

What Next?

Richard Lander returned to the Niger in 1832. His expedition was attacked and Lander was injured. He retreated to the island of Fernando Po, where he died.

Crossing the Sahara

Although Mungo Park had paddled past Timbuktu, it is unlikely he stopped at the city. It was closed to foreigners and its Muslim inhabitants would most probably have killed him and his crew. One Frenchman, however, was determined to visit this legendary "Queen of the Desert".

Travelling in disguise

René Caillié had twice visited west Africa and twice ended his journeys because of serious illness. The third time, in 1827, he was more successful. He disguised himself as an Egyptian Arab, which was easy as he was a fluent Arabic speaker. He then set off inland from Guinea with a small caravan of Mandingo traders heading for the Niger. Caillié said he was on his way home to Egypt and was treated well wherever he went.

René Caillié

As a child, René-Auguste Caillié (1799–1838) was obsessed with Africa. At 16, he became a cabin boy on a ship bound for the continent. He was later described as "one of the most reliable explorers of Africa".

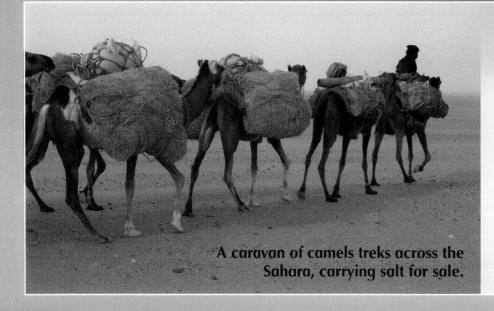

A caravan of camels treks across the Sahara, carrying salt for sale.

Desert trade

For centuries, vast caravans of traders have crossed the Sahara. They take precious goods such as gold and ostrich feathers from cities such as Timbuktu to north Africa. They return south with salt, cloth, glass, ceramics and horses.

Timbuktu

The city of Timbuktu lies a few hours' walk from the Niger. The city had once been a centre for the teaching of Islam. It was entirely dependent on the Niger trade and the cross-Sahara caravans, which were controlled by nomadic Tuareg traders.

A traditional clay building in Timbuktu.

Only expert guides can navigate through the vast sand dunes of the Sahara.

Timeline

April 1827
Caillié joins a trading caravan heading inland at Rio Nunez

11 June 1827
Reaches Timé, where he gets scurvy

9 January 1828
Leaves on a caravan heading for Djenné

23 March 1828
Sultan of Djenné gives Caillié a letter for Timbuktu merchants

20 April 1828
Enters Timbuktu

4 May 1828
Leaves Timbuktu and crosses the Sahara with a 1400-strong camel caravan

It's Amazing!
In 1826, Scottish explorer Alexander Gordon Laing became the first European to visit Timbuktu. He was murdered by his guide soon after he left.

The disappointing city

In Timé, south of the Niger, Caillié joined a caravan heading north to Djenné on the Niger. He then joined a cargo boat heading downstream to Timbuktu. He entered the forbidden city in April 1828, but was disappointed to find a collection of mud huts, not the fabulous city he had imagined. He left Timbuktu after two weeks, crossing the Sahara to Morocco and safety.

Into the desert

After Caillié had paved the way, Europeans began to flock to the previously unknown and unexplored Sahara. One of the most successful of this wave of explorers was a German called Heinrich Barth.

The urge to head south

In 1844, Barth arrived in Morocco and travelled east along the Mediterranean coast to Alexandria in Egypt. He learned a lot from this journey, but longed to head south into the desert. He returned to North Africa in 1850, this time intending to cross the Sahara. In Tripoli, Libya, he joined the English Mixed Scientific and Commercial Expedition, sponsored by the British government.

Heinrich Barth

Heinrich Barth (1821–65) found it hard to get on with other people. As a child, he was sent to North Africa by his father in an attempt to improve his social skills. This failed, but it did give the young Heinrich a taste for travel.

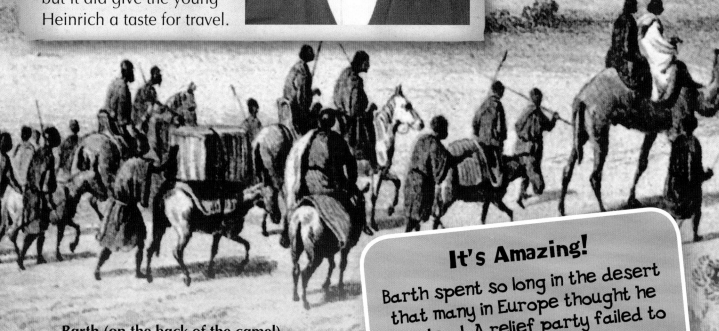

Barth (on the back of the camel) enters Timbuktu disguised as a holy man delivering religious books.

It's Amazing!

Barth spent so long in the desert that many in Europe thought he was dead. A relief party failed to find him, so his obituary was printed in the newspapers.

Timeline

March 1850
Barth joins expedition in Tripoli

April 1850
Discovers Roman ruins at Murzuq oasis

June 1850
Discovers Stone Age rock paintings in the Ahaggar mountains

April 1851
Explores area around Lake Chad

September 1853
Arrives in Timbuktu, where he stays for some months before returning to Lake Chad

September 1855
Arrives back in Tripoli

A Tuareg man wearing a tagelmust – a long cloth wrapped around the head and face.

The Tuareg

The Tuareg nomads of the mid 1800s survived the harsh conditions of the Sahara by raiding neighbouring tribes and demanding money from cross-Sahara caravans. At first, the Tuareg were hostile to Barth, but eventually they let him pass through the desert.

The learned explorer

Barth was a historian, linguist and geographer as well as an explorer. He made detailed records about the lands he travelled through. Barth discovered Stone Age paintings in the desert that showed it had once been fertile land. He recorded 40 native dialects around Lake Chad. He also visited Timbuktu, confirming Caillié's view of the city (see pages 170–71).

North meets south

In 1851, Barth stayed in the prosperous trading city of Kano in what is now northern Nigeria. It was the centre of extensive trading networks south to the coast, and north across the Sahara. Barth laid the groundwork for future European trade in the area.

The Kurmi market in Kano, founded in the 15th century and still used today.

Searching for the source

Much as the source and route of the River Niger preoccupied explorers in West Africa, the source of the River Nile fascinated explorers in East Africa. Everyone knew about its route through Egypt to the Mediterranean Sea, but where did this great river start?

James Bruce

Scotsman James Bruce (1730–94) started travelling after his wife died. He visited Spain and Portugal. When his father died four years later, he inherited enough money to travel full time. He first visited Africa in 1763.

Into Abyssinia

James Bruce was one of the first explorers to search for the source of the Nile. In 1768 he set off with about 20 men from Cairo up the Nile to the first set of cataracts (waterfalls) on the river at Aswan. He then headed east across the desert to the Red Sea. There he hired a ship to take him to Massawa, in what is now Eritrea. The party then headed inland to Gondar, capital of Abyssinia (now Ethiopia). Here he was granted the protection of the ruling emperor and helped in the country's civil war.

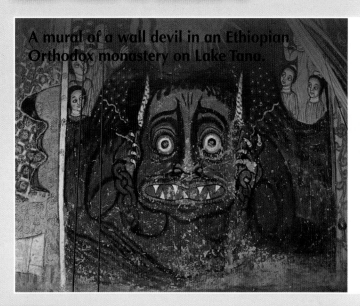

A mural of a wall devil in an Ethiopian Orthodox monastery on Lake Tana.

Land of monks

Lake Tana in northwest Ethiopia is fed by more than 60 streams, one of which is regarded as the source of the Blue Nile River. James Bruce recorded that there were as many as 45 inhabited islands on the lake, many with Christian monasteries on them.

1768
Bruce and 20 men set off from Cairo up the Nile to Aswan and then overland to the Red Sea

1769
Bruce sails down the Red Sea, stopping at Jeddah in Arabia before landing at Massawa and heading inland to Abyssinia

February 1770
Arrives in Gondar and gains protection from the Abyssinian emperor and his officials

November 1770
Reaches Lake Tana

At Lake Tana

From Gondar, Bruce headed south to Lake Tana, the source of the Blue Nile. Bruce considered the Blue Nile to be the main tributary of the Nile, so he thought he had discovered the source of the River Nile itself. In fact he was wrong, as the White Nile is the main tributary, but Bruce was elated: "… standing in that spot which had baffled the genius, industry and inquiry of both ancients and moderns for the course of near three thousand years. Though a mere private Briton, I have triumphed here."

The Blue Nile Falls, where the Blue Nile empties out of Lake Tana.

What Next?
When Bruce returned home, many people thought he had made up his stories about his journey. He was only believed when others visited the region.

To Lake Victoria

The Ancient Greeks believed that the River Nile began in high mountains. In 1848, a German missionary saw a snow-capped mountain near the Equator. This was the volcanic mountain Kilimanjaro. It was nothing to do with the Nile, but sparked interest in the source of the river.

The wrong lake

In 1856, the Royal Geographical Society in London sent an expedition to solve the mystery once and for all. Richard Burton and John Speke trekked from Zanzibar inland to Kazeh (Tabora) in western Tanzania. From here, they headed west to Ujiji on the shores of Lake Tanganyika. Burton had been convinced this was the source of the Nile, but found that no river flowed north out of the lake.

Richard Burton

Richard Burton (1821–90) was a controversial figure in the 19th century. He published more than 50 books, including a frank translation of the often raunchy Arabic tales *The Arabian Nights*.

John Hanning Speke

John Hanning Speke (1827–64) left home at 17 to join the British Indian Army. He spent most of his leave exploring the Himalayas. Speke first met Burton during an expedition to Somalia in 1854. He came close to death when tribesmen attacked them, but recovered to join Burton on their second expedition in 1857.

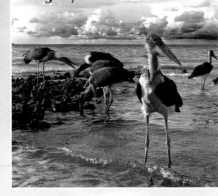

Marabou storks feed on the shores of Lake Tanganyika.

Lake Tanganyika

When Burton and Speke discovered Lake Tanganyika in 1858, only Burton saw it because disease had left Speke temporarily blind. The second largest lake in Africa, after Victoria, water from it flows via the Lukaga and Congo rivers to the Atlantic.

Finding Lake Victoria

The pair returned to Kazeh and then split up, Speke heading north. In July 1858 he discovered Lake Victoria and, although he had little proof, he was convinced the lake was the true source of the Nile. Speke reported his findings to the Royal Geographical Society, who agreed to fund another expedition.

Timeline

17 June 1857
Burton and Speke head west from Zanzibar

December 1857
They set out for Ujiji

13 February 1858
Reach Lake Tanganyika

April 1858
Burton rests in Ujiji and Speke heads north

30 July 1858
Speke reaches Lake Victoria

1859
Back in London, Speke presents his theory about the source of the Nile before Burton, who disputes it, has returned from Africa

Fishermen in Lake Victoria, or Ukerewe, a vital source of food for the large population that lives near it.

What Next?

The local people called the lake Ukerewe, but Speke named it Lake Victoria in honour of the British queen.

Mission accomplished

John Speke was sure he had found the source of the Nile in Lake Victoria in 1858. But some back in London wanted more proof, so he returned to Africa to find it.

The true source of the Nile

Speke set off in 1860 accompanied by James Grant. They travelled round the western edge of Lake Victoria. Grant was forced to rest due to an infected leg, so was not with Speke in July 1862 when he found a waterfall at the northern end of the lake. It led down to a river – this was the start of the Nile.

James Grant

James Grant (1827–92) met John Speke while serving in the British army in India. After Speke's death, Grant defended his friend's achievements until Henry Stanley proved Speke right in 1875 (see pages 186–87).

Grant and Speke negotiate a safe passage with the Queen Dowager of Uganda.

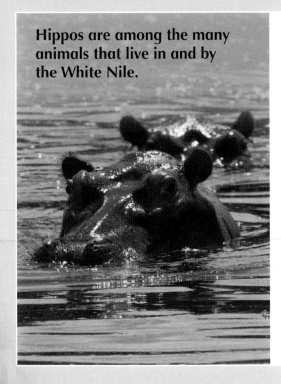

Hippos are among the many animals that live in and by the White Nile.

The White Nile

The most distant stream of the White Nile (the major tributary of the Nile) starts in the Nyungwe Forest in southern Rwanda. It flows out of Lake Victoria and then north until it meets the Blue Nile at Khartoum. The river gets its name from the particles of whitish clay suspended in its waters.

Timeline

April 1860
Speke and Grant depart for East Africa

1861
Reach Kaweh and head north round western edge of Lake Victoria; Grant falls ill

28 July 1862
Speke discovers and names the Ripon Falls

February 1863
The two arrive in Gondokoro in Sudan, and meet Samuel and Florence Baker

March 1864
The Bakers discover the Murchison Falls and Lake Albert

15 September 1864
Speke accidentally shoots himself

A tragic accident

Back in London, Speke and Grant were treated as heroes. But not everyone was convinced they had found the source of the Nile. Their most prominent critic was Richard Burton, who insisted that they had not proved that the river emerged from Lake Victoria. The pair agreed to debate the issue in public. The day before the debate, however, Speke accidentally shot himself.

Filling in the gaps

The Royal Geographical Society asked Samuel and Florence Baker to search for Speke and Grant, who had not been heard of for a year. After finding them, the Bakers explored parts of the Nile that Speke had not visited. They found that the river flows from Lake Victoria down through the Murchison Falls before heading north into Sudan.

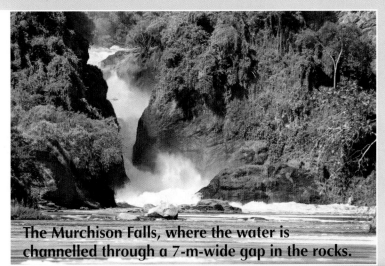

The Murchison Falls, where the water is channelled through a 7-m-wide gap in the rocks.

Livingstone in Africa

David Livingstone was first and foremost a doctor and missionary, but he was also a superb explorer. The books he wrote about his four great journeys brought Africa to European attention. His fight against the Arab-run slave trade eventually ended that cruel practice.

It's Amazing!

In 1844, Livingstone was almost killed by a lion that "shook me as a terrier does a rat". He was left with many broken bones and 11 tooth marks in his left arm.

Timeline

14 March 1841
Livingstone lands in Cape Town

1841–44
Explores Kalahari Desert

June 1849
Discovers Lake Ngami

April 1851
Discovers Zambezi

November 1853
Sets off west from the Zambesi

31 May 1854
Reaches Luanda in Angola then heads east

20 May 1856
Reaches Quelimane on Indian Ocean

August 1859
Discovers Lake Nyasa on third expedition

First journey

Livingstone arrived in Cape Town in 1841. He headed inland to work at a Christian mission at Kuruman at the edge of the Kalahari Desert. Three years later, he moved farther north to set up his own mission. He took every opportunity to explore the area. He became the first European to see Lake Ngami in northern Botswana and, in 1851, the Zambezi – a previously unknown river. At this point, he accompanied his wife and four children back to Cape Town to send them back to England.

David Livingstone

Dr David Livingstone (1813–73) was born into a poor family in Blantyre, Scotland. At the age of just 10 he was working 14 hours a day in a local cotton mill. He later worked part-time in the mill while studying to be a doctor in Glasgow so that he could become a medical missionary.

1841–49
1850–56
1858–64
1865–73
(see pages 183–84)

Nyangwe

Ujiji

Tabora

Zanzibar

Lake Tanganyika

Lake Mweru

River Ruvuma

Central
Africa

Lake Bangweulu

Lake Nyasa

River Zambezi

River Zambezi

Sesheke

River Zambezi

Quelimane

Victoria Falls

Luanda

Lake Ngami

Indian
Ocean

Kalahari
Desert

Across the continent

Back on the Zambezi in 1853, Livingstone set off to find a route to the Atlantic Ocean. He hoped that by opening the continent up to European influence and development, the slave trade might be ended. He reached the coast then turned round and canoed down the Zambezi to Quelimane on the Indian Ocean. On a third expedition to explore the Zambezi, he discovered Lake Nyasa.

Orange River

Kuruman

Atlantic
Ocean

Cape Town

Dr Livingstone, I presume?

In 1865, David Livingstone set out on his fourth and final journey. This time his aim was to find the source of three great African rivers: the Congo, Zambezi and Nile. John Speke had discovered the Nile's source, but many still doubted him. Livingstone set off to find out for himself.

A futile search

Livingstone started his journey on the River Ruvuma – the boundary between Tanzania and Mozambique – before trekking north to Lake Tanganyika. He spent the next three years exploring this and other lakes in the region and trying to work out which one was the source of the Nile. In fact none was, as most of them drained into the Congo.

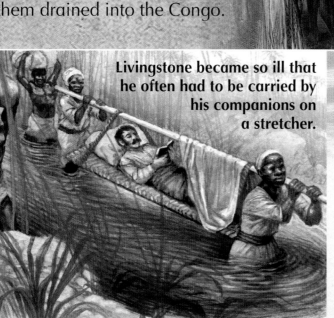

Livingstone became so ill that he often had to be carried by his companions on a stretcher.

The final journey

By the end of his life, Livingstone was weak with fever and becoming increasingly confused. For the first time ever, he got lost when his chronometers were accidentally damaged, and his sextant developed a fault. But he was still driven to travel in his quest to end the slave trade.

A 19th-century painting based on Livingstone's description of the moment he and Stanley first met.

Lechwe, a kind of antelope, near Lake Bangweulu, where Livingstone died.

Livingstone's end

When Livingstone died, his companions, Chuma and Susi carried his body over 1000 km to the coast so that it could be taken back to Britain. As he had requested, his heart was buried under a tree in a village near Lake Bangweulu.

Timeline

22 March 1866
Livingstone lands on East African coast

8 August 1866
Reaches Lake Nyasa

1 April 1867
Livingstone reaches Lake Tanganyika

November 1867
Reaches Lake Mweru

18 July 1868
First sees Lake Bangweulu

29 March 1871
Arrives in Nyangwe, the most northerly point in his travels

10 November 1871
Meets Stanley at Ujiji

1 May 1873
Livingstone dies near Lake Bangweulu

A famous meeting

Livingstone had been out of touch with the rest of the world since 1869, so in 1871 an American newspaper hired Henry Stanley to seek him out. The pair met on 10 November 1871 at Ujiji. Stanley later reported that he was so overwhelmed, he took off his hat and uttered the famous words: "Dr Livingstone, I presume?"

Livingstone's legacy

Although Livingstone did not discover the source of any major river, end the slave trade or establish permanent missions, he did add a vast amount to European knowledge of Africa. He discovered several lakes and charted the Zambezi and other rivers. Soon after his death, the slave trade dramatically declined.

A statue of Livingstone at Victoria Falls.

What Next?

A month after Livingstone's death, the British closed down the slave market in Zanzibar, the busiest in Africa.

Meeting Stanley

By 1871, Dr Livingstone had been in Africa for 30 years and had travelled many thousands of kilometres. He was old, ill, and unable to cope with the lengthy marches from place to place. His servants often had to carry him on a stretcher, but he was determined to press on. In this extract from his diary, Livingstone describes his feelings on first meeting Stanley.

Returning to Ujiji

23 SEPTEMBER We now crossed the River Longumba twice and then came near the great mountain mass on the west of Lake Tanganyika. From here to Tanganyika is about ten days' march through open forest. I was sorely ill by this march back to Ujiji. By the end of it I felt as if dying on my feet. Almost every step in pain, my appetite failed, while my mind, sorely depressed, acted on my body.

8 OCTOBER The road covered with fragments of quartz was very sore to my feet, which were crammed into ill-made French shoes. How the bare feet of the men and women stood out, I don't know.

The 'good Samaritan'

NOVEMBER— When my spirits were at their lowest ebb, the good Samaritan was close at hand, for one morning Susi came running at the top of his speed and gasped out, "An Englishman, I see him!" and off he darted to meet him.

The American flag at the head of the caravan told me of the nationality of the stranger. Baths of tin, huge kettles, cooking pots and tents made me think "This must be a luxurious traveller, and not one at his wits' end like me." It was Henry Moreland Morton Stanley, the traveling correspondent to the New York Herald. He had been sent by James Gordon Bennett, at an expense of more than 4000 pounds, to find out accurate information about me, and if dead to bring home my bones. The news he had to tell to one who had been two full years without any tidings from Europe made my whole frame thrill.

Appetite returned, and instead of the spare, tasteless two meals a day I ate four times daily, and in a week began to feel strong. But this kindness of Mr Bennett, so nobly carried into effect by Mr Stanley, was simply overwhelming. I really do feel extremely grateful, and at the same time I am a little ashamed at not being more worthy of the generosity.

The exploration of the Congo

Henry Stanley was a very different man from Livingstone. He was an adventurer, not an explorer, interested solely in fame and fortune. Livingstone often travelled almost alone, but Stanley commanded large, armed groups.

Across Africa

Stanley set off in 1874 to explore the River Congo. He left from Zanzibar and headed to Lake Victoria, which he sailed round in a collapsible canoe, the *Lady Alice*. He sailed down the Congo, often coming under attack from hostile locals and setting fire to their villages in revenge. In 1877, he reached the Atlantic coastline and sent stories of his trip to European newspapers.

Stanley's boat, the *Lady Alice*, was collapsible so that it could be carried around rapids.

Henry Stanley

Henry Morton Stanley (1841–1904) was born John Rowlands in North Wales. He moved to New Orleans in his teens, and eventually took a job as a reporter for the *New York Herald*, who sent him to find Livingstone.

Settling the Congo

Stanley colonized the Congo on behalf of Leopold II of Belgium. He negotiated treaties with local chiefs and explored the lands either side of the river. He earned the nickname 'Bula Matari' – 'Rock Breaker' – for his harsh treatment of those who worked for him.

A chief of the Molunga, a tribe who signed a treaty with Stanley, which they were later to regret under Leopold II's harsh rule.

Timeline

14 March 1872
Stanley leaves Livingstone

1874
Sets out from Zanzibar

January 1875
Reaches Lake Victoria

October 1876
Reaches River Lualaba and heads down river

August 1877
Reaches Atlantic coast

1879–84
Colonizes the Congo

1888
Finds Emin Pasha at Lake Albert

What Next?

Leopold II ran the Congo Free State. The Belgian government forced him to hand it over in 1908 due to his terrible treatment of its people. The country gained its independence in 1960.

Stanley the colonialist

King Leopold II paid Stanley to colonize the Congo as he was desperate to have an African colony. Stanley did this in five years from 1879, creating the Congo Free State. On his final mission, Stanley rescued Emin Pasha, the governor of southern Sudan, who was under siege from rebel forces.

A goliath tigerfish, one of the many dangerous fish that live in the River Congo.

The River Congo

The vast River Congo starts as the River Lualaba in the mountains of southern Congo, and then flows for 4700 km in a great loop until it reaches the Atlantic Ocean. Rapids near its mouth make it difficult to access from the sea.

A woman alone

Almost without exception, the explorers of Africa were men. Mary Kingsley, however, broke all the rules of her time and became one of the most important explorers of West Africa.

The late starter

Kingsley was the daughter of a widely travelled doctor, but she herself had rarely left home before her first expedition to Africa. She had no formal education, so she asked the British Museum which natural history subjects she should study. They suggested she collect specimens of beetles and fish. She quickly learned navigation and other skills, and fell in love with the people of Africa.

Timeline

August 1893
Kingsley sets sail from England on board the cargo ship *Lagos*, reaching as far south as Angola

January 1894
Returns to the UK, where the British Museum agree to fund her next expedition

November 1894
Explores the River Ogowe in Gabon before trekking to the River Rembwe

September 1895
Climbs Mt Cameroon

November 1895
Returns to London and writes about her travels

Kingsley travelled in full Victorian dress and carried an umbrella, which she used to scare off nosy hippos!

Mary Kingsley

Mary Kingsley (1862–1900) spent most of her life at home caring for her invalid mother. Only when her parents both died was she able to fulfil her desire to travel. After her two explorations, she returned to Africa to nurse British soldiers in the Boer War and died of fever.

Earning respect

Kingsley's first expedition down the west coast of Africa proved her worth as an explorer, and the British Museum agreed to support another expedition in 1894. She became the first person to travel through much of Gabon and the first woman to climb Mt Cameroon. Kingsley often travelled alone, trading with local tribes. She always made sure she never drank unboiled water, which kept her free from many diseases.

The foothills of Mount Cameroon, which Mary Kingsley climbed in 1895.

It's a Mystery!

When she climbed Mount Cameroon, Kingsley's guides deserted her midway, so she made the final ascent by herself.

Kingsley studied the belief systems of African shamans, or holy men.

Enlightened traveller

Mary Kingsley did not share the racist views of many of her fellow European explorers. She was therefore better able to understand the African cultures she studied. She insisted that Africans were every bit as cultured and advanced as Europeans.

Wildlife adventures

Kingsley seemed to be fearless of the risks she faced, both from the people she encountered and from the continent's dangerous animals. She hit an attacking leopard over the head with a water pot and rescued another from a trap. She also had close encounters with crocodiles.

Kingsley was not put off by Africa's dangerous wildlife, including leopards.

EXTREME EXPLORATION

By the start of the 20th century, most of the world's land had been explored and mapped. However, the polar regions remained unconquered. Explorers also found new challenges: diving in the oceans and descending to their greatest depths, and climbing the highest mountains. With the arrival of space travel, we have been able to explore our moon and, using unmanned craft, our solar system and the stars beyond it.

The race to the North Pole

By the middle of the 19th century, the coastline of the Arctic Ocean was known to explorers. But they had yet to reach the very top of the world – the North Pole. The race to get there first soon began in earnest.

Fridtjof Nansen

Norwegian Nansen (1861–1930) was a skilled Arctic explorer who planned his missions with great care. He became a diplomat in later life and was awarded the Nobel Prize for Peace in 1922.

Ever further north

One of the first Polar explorers was the American Charles Hall (1821–71) who, during three expeditions, sailed further north than anyone before. He was the first person to visit the north shore of Greenland. Hall used the techniques of the local Inuit to help him survive, but fell ill and died on board his ship *Polaris*.

The *Fram* was built to withstand the pressure of the ice.

The reinforced ship

In 1884, objects from a ship that had sunk off Siberia were found on the other side of the Arctic Ocean in Greenland. They were carried there by currents in the Arctic Ocean. This find gave Nansen the idea of floating to the North Pole. His ship, the *Fram*, was specially built using thick wood reinforced with metal.

A tragic flight

Swedish engineer Salomon Andrée (1854–97) tried to fly to the North Pole in a hot-air balloon. In July 1897, he took off from Spitsbergen in his balloon *Ornen* (*Eagle*), but disappeared after two days. The wreckage of the balloon and the bodies of Andrée and his two companions were found on the ice.

Andrée and his co-pilots stand in front of their balloon on Spitsbergen.

Floating in the ice

In 1893, Fridtjof Nansen set out on his remarkable expedition. He sailed his ship, the *Fram*, into the pack ice and hoped that the Arctic currents would take his ice-bound ship to the North Pole. The ship remained frozen in for two years before Nansen realized it would miss the Pole. He and a companion then tried unsuccessfully to walk the rest of the way.

Ice forms a solid mass across much of the Arctic Ocean.

It's Amazing!

While on the Fram, Nansen found that the Arctic Ocean was both much deeper and warmer than expected. He proved there was no land mass under the North Pole.

Timeline

August 1871
Hall sails up the west coast of Greenland and sledges 320 km across the pack ice towards the North Pole

26 June 1893
Nansen sets sail on the *Fram*

20 September 1893
The *Fram* is frozen in and pushed northeast by the ocean current

14 March 1895
Nansen and Frederick Johansen set off with dogsleds, reaching further north than anyone else before, but are forced to turn back

July 1897
Andrée attempts to fly to the North Pole in a hot-air balloon

Reaching the Pole

The race for the North Pole carried on into the early years of the 20th century. It was eventually won by the American explorer Robert Peary in 1909. Controversy continues to rage around his achievement, however, with some historians doubting he ever reached the Pole at all.

Preparing for the Pole

In a series of expeditions starting in 1886, Robert Peary pushed further north. Each time he learned more about how to survive in the Arctic. By 1909, he was ready for the final attempt. The clothes, sleeping quarters, food, dogs and sledges had all been chosen specially for this expedition. The 24-man team left base camp on Ellesmere Island in March 1909, and set up a series of supply camps along two-thirds of the route to the Pole.

Robert Peary

Robert Peary (1836–1920) devoted himself to Arctic exploration for a quarter of a century. He had trained as a civil engineer and worked for the navy before beginning his Arctic quest. He paid for his expeditions by writing about his adventures in books and magazines.

Matthew Henson

Matthew Henson (1866–1955) was an African American born into poverty. At first, Henson worked for Peary as a valet but he soon took responsibility for organizing his expeditions.

Racing there and back

The expedition made good time over the hard ice, allowing Peary, Henson and four local Inuit to make the final 250 km to the Pole. After five days, on 6 April 1909 they set up camp just 5 km short of the Pole. They crossed the Pole the next day before heading back to Cape Columbia, covering 112 km in one day. Some doubted that Peary could have travelled at the speed he did.

This drawing was made from a photograph taken by Peary of the four Inuit in the team that reached the Pole.

Timeline

April 1908
Peary and his expedition drop anchor near Cape Sheridan on Ellesmere Island; they then build a base camp further north at Cape Columbia

1 March 1909
The expedition leaves base camp

2 April 1909
Peary, Henson and four Inuit make the final dash to the Pole

6 April 1909
Establish camp just short of the Pole

7 April 1909
Peary stays in the area for 30 hours to make the calculations to prove he is at the Pole

23 April 1909
Peary and team return to base camp

What Next?
If Peary did not really reach the Pole, the first man who did was the British explorer Wally Herbert in 1969.

The first exploration of Antarctica

Captain Cook sailed into Antarctic waters in 1773 but this vast, cold, inhospitable continent remained virtually unseen for another 70 years. Its landmass was hard to find, as it was overlapped with a huge ice sheet that spread out into the sea.

Carstens Borchgrevink

Norwegian Carstens Borchgrevink (1864–1934) was the first person to land on Antarctica. As part of a group searching for new whaling waters, he landed near Cape Adare in Victoria Land on 24 January 1895.

Breaking through the ice

Sir James Ross (1800–62) was a hugely experienced English polar explorer. In 1841 he managed to steer his two ships, the *Terror* and *Erebus*, through the pack ice that surrounds the continent. He then sailed into the sea that is now named after him, but he was unable to land on the continent itself.

Ross and his crew land on Possession Island.

Ice and fire

On 12 January 1841, James Ross came close to Antarctica when he landed on an icy island off Victoria Land. He named it Possession Island. Two weeks later he sighted an active volcano, which he named Mt Erebus.

An Antarctic winter

In February 1899, Carstens Borchgrevink arrived off Cape Adare on board the *Southern Cross*, a Norwegian whaling ship. He landed with a small scientific team, including a meteorologist and a naturalist. His team also included two Lapps from northern Norway, who were experts at surviving in cold conditions.
The team built a hut and survived a whole winter in the continent.

A drawing made by cook Kolbein Ellefsen in the hut where the team spent the winter.

Ross's ships HMS *Terror* and HMS *Erebus* sail past Mt Erebus.

Timeline

1820
Two separate ships sight Antarctica

9 January 1841
Ross's two ships breach the pack ice and he discovers Victoria Land

28 January 1841
Ross sights an active volcano on Ross Island

24 January 1895
Borchgrevink sets foot on Antarctica

1899
Borchgrevink and a scientific team spend winter in Antarctica

Race to the Pole

With the North Pole reached in 1909, only the South Pole remained unconquered. Its harsh, unforgiving climate had already defeated several expeditions, but in 1910 two well-equipped teams set out for the Pole. It was to be a race to the death.

The race begins

The first team was led by Roald Amundsen, the Norwegian hero of the northwest passage (see pages 78–79). Leaving the Bay of Whales on the east side of the Ross Sea on 19 October 1911, he headed across the ice shelf and up to the polar plateau. Just under two weeks later, a British expedition led by Robert Scott set out from the western end of the Ross Sea in McMurdo Sound and made their way on to the plateau.

Robert Scott

Captain Scott (1868–1912) was already an experienced Antarctic explorer by the time he set off for the Pole in 1911. He had taken part in a major expedition with Ernest Shackleton in 1901–04.

A heavy load

Robert Scott's expedition was not as well prepared as Amundsen's, and relied mainly on Siberian ponies to pull their supplies. The ponies soon died of cold, forcing his team to pull the supplies on skis. Amundsen used skills learned from the Inuit in the Arctic, and took huskies instead.

Scott's party pull their heavy sleds across the ice.

SOUTH POLE

Scott's last supply depot
14 January 1912

Amundsen's last supply depot
8 December 1911

Polar Plateau

Transantarctic Mountains

A N T A R C T I C A

Ross Ice Shelf

Scott's last camp
19 March 1912

Bay of Whales

McMurdo Sound

ROSS SEA

Timeline

19 October 1911
Amundsen's team sets off from Bay of Whales

1 November 1911
Scott's team leave their base by McMurdo Sound

14 December 1911
Amundsen and team reach the South Pole

11 January 1912
Amundsen returns to base camp

17 January 1912
Scott reaches the Pole

17 March 1912
The sick Captain Oates walks out of the camp to die in the snow

29 March 1912
Scott and two remaining companions die

A Norwegian triumph

Amundsen's better preparations gave him the edge over Scott. His team arrived first at the Pole on 14 December 1911. They were back at their base camp by the time Scott reached the Pole on 17 January 1912. Tired and despondent, Scott and his team all died on the return journey, the last three within just 18 km of safety.

Amundsen's team

Scott's team

Crossing Antarctica

Ernest Shackleton attempted to reach the South Pole in 1908. He and his team managed to get to the Magnetic South Pole (the place magnets point to, 180 km from the geographic South Pole), then turned back. In 1915, he returned with an even more ambitious plan.

Ernest Shackleton

Shackelton (1874–1922) first went to the Antarctic in 1901. After his two expeditions of 1908 and 1915, he returned in 1921 to explore Enderby Land, but died in South Georgia before he could reach it.

Coast to coast

Shackleton's plan was to cross the continent from the Weddell Sea to the Ross Sea. But it almost failed before it started, as World War I broke out in Europe just as he was about to set sail from England. Shackleton offered his two ships, *Endurance* and *Aurora*, for war duty, but was instructed to continue with his expedition.

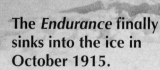

The *Endurance* finally sinks into the ice in October 1915.

Mawson's disaster

In 1911, Douglas Mawson led an Australian expedition to explore the Antarctic coastline. One of his team plunged into a crack in the ice with almost all the food. Mawson reached base camp only to find the supply ship had just left. He was only rescued at the end of the winter.

Mawson and companion Xavier Mertz struggle through the snow.

Trapped

The *Endurance* arrived in the Weddell Sea in January 1915, and was immediately trapped in pack ice. After 10 months, it sank. Shackleton and his party sailed to Elephant Island in the lifeboats. From there, he and five others set sail to seek help. They reached South Georgia and returned to rescue the rest of his team.

It's Amazing!
Shackleton never lost a single man in the Antarctic, a rare achievement in polar exploration.

One of the snow tractors used by Fuchs to cross Antarctica.

Success!

Antarctica was finally crossed from coast to coast in 1958 when an expedition led by Vivian Fuchs crossed from the Weddell to the Ross seas. He used snow tractors and had the benefit of ice-breakers, radios, heaters and a base at the South Pole itself – none of which were available to Shackleton.

Timeline

December 1913
Mawson is rescued after surviving two Antarctic winters

January 1915
Endurance enters the Weddell Sea, where it is trapped in pack ice

27 October 1915
Endurance sinks and the crew sail to Elephant Island

30 August 1916
Shackleton returns to rescue the expedition on Elephant Island

2 March 1958
Fuchs completes first successful crossing of Antarctica

Shackleton's Antarctic diary

In 1908 Ernest Shackleton and three others attempted to reach the South Pole, but stopped 155 km short. They were the first humans to reach the Polar plateau. These are extracts from Shackleton's diary.

DECEMBER 30

We only did 4 miles 100 yards today. We started at 7 am but had to camp at 11 am, a blizzard springing up from the south. It is very annoying.

DECEMBER 31

The hardest day we have had, pushing through soft snow uphill with a strong head wind and drift all day. We are all feeling bad for lack of food.

JANUARY 4
The end is in
sight. We can
only go for
three more days
at the most, for we are
weakening rapidly. Short food and
a blizzard wind from the south, with
driving drift, have plainly told us
today that we are reaching our limit.

JANUARY 6
This must be our last outward march with
the sledge and camp equipment. Tomorrow we
must leave camp with some food, and push
as far south as possible.

JANUARY 9
Our last day outwards. We looked
south, but could see nothing but
the dead white snow plain.

203

John Murray

Canadian John Murray (1844–1914) served as Charles Thomson's assistant on the *Challenger* expedition. He edited and published the 50 volumes of reports that appeared later.

The voyage of the *Challenger*

Oceans cover seven tenths of the Earth, but before the mid 1800s surprisingly little was known about what lay beneath the surface. In 1872, a remarkable expedition set sail to investigate on a ship that had been specially adapted for scientific research.

Scientists at work in the biology laboratory on the *Challenger*.

Floating laboratory

The idea for the expedition came from Charles Wyville Thomson (1830–92), professor of zoology at Edinburgh University. He persuaded the Royal Navy to loan him HMS *Challenger*, a steam-powered warship. Her guns and some masts were removed to make more room for laboratories and cabins, and a dredging platform was added to take samples from the sea floor.

The diving bell

In 1690, Edmund Halley invented a bell that allowed divers to work under water. The wooden bell was covered with lead to make it sink and filled with air pumped down through leather pipes from the surface. Four people could stay down at a depth of 18 m for 90 minutes.

A wealth of knowledge

The *Challenger* set sail in 1872 and remained at sea for four years, crossing every ocean except the Arctic. During the course of the expedition, it sailed 127,500 km and discovered 4717 new species of marine life. When its reports were published, their editor, John Murray, described them as "the greatest advance in knowledge of our planet since the celebrated discoveries of the 15th century".

Diving suits

One of the first diving suits was invented in 1797 by the German C H Kleingert, who enclosed the diver's upper body in a cylinder. Later suits allowed the diver to swim around more easily. Air was pumped to the diver inside a heavy metal helmet. The pressure of the air escaping from the helmet prevented water from flooding into it.

Timeline

1690
Edmund Halley invents the diving bell

1797
C H Kleingert invents early, rigid diving suit

1819
August Siebe invents a more flexible suit with a heavy metal helmet

1855
First textbook on oceanography (science of the oceans) published

21 December 1872
HMS *Challenger* sets sail from Portsmouth

1876
Challenger expedition ends

To the bottom of the oceans

It is difficult for divers to operate deep under the sea, as the pressure on a diver's lungs is intense and the water is cold and dark. As a result, the deep seas remained almost entirely unknown until a new invention made underwater exploration possible in the 1930s.

Timeline

6 June 1930
The bathysphere makes its first deep-sea dive off Nonsuch Island in Bermuda

1934
Barton and Beebe make a world record descent of 923 m off Bermuda, a record that stands for 15 years

1953
The bathyscaphe *Trieste* is launched in Italy

23 January 1960
With Auguste Piccard's son Jacques and Don Walsh of the US Navy on board, the *Trieste* reaches the ocean floor of the Challenger Deep – the deepest part of the Mariana Trench

The bathysphere

The bathysphere was developed in 1930 by two Americans – the scientist William Beebe and the diver Otis Barton. It consisted of a metal sphere lowered into the water on a steel cable attached to a surface ship. Once they are sealed inside, the divers breathe oxygen from a high-pressure cylinder. They made their first descent in the waters off Bermuda in 1930.

William Beebe (left) and Otis Barton next to the bathysphere.

William Beebe

William Beebe (1877–1962) was curator of ornithology at the New York Zoological Society, but he was interested in far more than just birds. He made 35 dives in the bathysphere to observe the marine life of the Atlantic Ocean.

The view of the Atlantic Ocean floor from a modern deep-sea craft.

Deep-sea life

Explorers have discovered many amazing and previously unknown creatures in the deep oceans, such as the anglerfish (below). These strange creatures exist in total darkness, eating scraps that sink down from the surface.

The bathyscaphe

In 1953, Swiss scientist Auguste Piccard (1884–1962) developed the bathyscaphe. This craft used a system of floodable tanks to move independently in even the deepest waters. In 1960, the *Trieste* bathyscaphe reached the deepest part of the world's oceans, the Challenger Deep in the Pacific Ocean, 10,911 m below sea level.

The world beneath the waves

Just below the ocean waves is a beautiful world of fish, sea mammals, coral reefs and marine plant life. Until very recently that world was closed to us. One man more than any other made it possible for people to explore beneath the waves.

A portable air supply

In 1943 the French underwater explorer Jacques Cousteau, working with the engineer Emile Gagnan, invented the aqualung, a portable air supply carried on a diver's back. The invention enabled Cousteau to explore the underwater world, taking photographs of the wonderful sights he saw.

It's Amazing!

Cousteau was fascinated by the idea of living underwater. In 1963, he built an underwater house in the Red Sea and lived in it for a month.

Thanks to Cousteau, divers are able to experience the beauty of coral reefs, such as this one in the Red Sea.

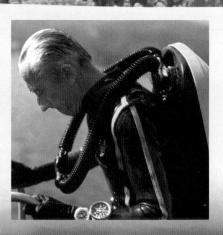

Jacques Cousteau

French naval officer Jacques-Yves Cousteau (1910–97) became fascinated by the water at an early age. After World War II, when he fought for the French Resistance, he set up his own underwater research company.

The *Calypso*'s condition is deteriorating as Cousteau's relatives argue over its fate.

A disputed legacy

Cousteau's boat *Calypso* was built for the British Royal Navy. He turned it into a base for his diving. Since Cousteau's death, ownership of the *Calypso* has been disputed and it has not been used.

Revealing a new world

Cousteau's underwater photography of the coral reefs of the Red Sea was the first detailed investigation of sea life. His 1956 film *The Silent World* was the first colour underwater film to be shown to a wide audience. Throughout his life, Cousteau was interested in educating people about the underwater environment. In 1985, he began a long-term research project to examine the health of the world's oceans and seas.

A diver explores inside a shipwreck with the help of an aqualung.

The aqualung

The aqualung was the world's first self-contained diving unit. The high-pressure air supply is carried on the diver's back in cylinders, and reaches the diver via a tube connected to a mouthpiece. The aqualung allows divers to swim freely to a depth of 30 metres without restrictive cables or a heavy diving suit.

Timeline

1938
Cousteau first dives in the Mediterranean

1943
Invents the aqualung with Emile Gagnan

1950
Acquires the *Calypso*

1952–53
Makes pioneering photographic study of the Red Sea

1963
Lives underwater for a month

1973
Founds Cousteau Society for the Protection of Ocean Life

1985
Starts research project into the state of the world's oceans

The top of the world

The high mountains of the Himalayas in Asia have long fascinated European explorers. Different nations concentrated on different Himalayan peaks: the Germans on Nanga Parbat, the Italians on K2 – the second highest mountain in the world – and the British on Everest – the highest of them all.

Preparing the way

In the years after the end of World War I in 1918, 13 expeditions attempted – and failed – to reach the summit of Everest, all from the Tibetan side. In 1949, Nepal opened up its borders to Europeans, allowing climbers to tackle Everest from its side of the border. The following year, French climbers reached the top of Annapurna I, breaking the psychological 8000 metre barrier. The way was now clear to tackle Everest.

Timeline

10 March 1953
Expedition led by John Hunt leaves Katmandu and treks through the Himalayan foothills

25 March
Expedition sets up base camp on the Khunbu glacier at 5530 m

28 May
Hillary and Tenzing set off with a support team that turns back at 8590 m

29 May
Hillary and Tenzing reach the summit at 11.30 am and spend 15 minutes there before descending

Tenzing and Hillary

Tenzing Norgay (1914– 86), left, was a Nepalese with a vast experience of Himalayan climbing. He reached to within 250 metres of the summit with a Swiss expedition in 1952. Edmund Hillary (born 1919), right, was born in Auckland, New Zealand, and climbed his first major mountain aged 20. In 1950, he climbed in the Alps and made his first visit to the Himalayas in 1951.

Reaching the summit

The expedition in 1953 was carefully planned, with a series of supply camps established up to the South Crest at 8550 m. From there, two climbers would climb the final 300 m to the summit. Accompanied by a support group, Edmund Hillary and Tenzing Norgay set out on 28 May, spending that night on a narrow, snow-covered ledge. The next morning was clear, allowing the pair to climb to the summit.

A supply camp on a modern expedition to climb Everest.

Mount Everest, at 8850 metres, is the highest mountain in the world.

It's Amazing!

Since the conquest of Everest in 1953, the mountain has been climbed almost every year. Fifty-four climbers reached the summit on one day, 15 May 2002.

Supply camps

The 1953 expedition established a series of nine camps between base camp at the foot of the Khunbu glacier and the summit. Each camp was supplied with food and equipment necessary for the climb, including oxygen tanks for the climbers.

Mountain guides

Tenzing Norgay was a Sherpa. The Sherpa are an ethnic group from the Himalayan region of Nepal. Their ancestors migrated to Nepal from eastern Tibet about 500 years ago. The Sherpa are tough, hardy people well used to the high altitudes of the Himalayas, and they are valuable guides and porters on mountaineering expeditions in the region.

The Sherpa are used to making long journeys on foot at high altitudes.

Into space

The attention of many potential explorers turned towards the heavens and into space after 1945. The technological advances required to send a man into orbit round the world, let alone to the Moon, and then bring him safely back to Earth were immense.

The Space Race

Near the end of World War II, Germany had developed the technology to fire V-2 rockets at supersonic speeds within the Earth's atmosphere. Once the war ended, scientists used this technology to build rockets capable of escaping the Earth's gravity and travelling through space. A competition began between the USA and the USSR (now Russia) to put a man into space.

Timeline

4 October 1957
USSR launches the world's first artificial satellite, *Sputnik I*

November 1957
A dog called Laika is the first living creature in space on *Sputnik II*, but dies in orbit

20 August 1960
Sputnik V carries two dogs into orbit, and brings them back to Earth safely

12 April 1961
Yuri Gagarin becomes the first person in space, orbiting the Earth once on board *Vostok I*

Yuri Gagarin

Yuri Gagarin (1934–68) was born in western Russia, and qualified as a military pilot in 1957. He was chosen along with 19 other cosmonauts to join the Soviet space programme in 1960. His successful space flight in 1961 made him into an international celebrity. He died on a military training flight seven years later.

Two firsts

The USSR launched the world's first artificial satellite (object that orbits the Earth), *Sputnik I*, in 1957. Four years later, cosmonaut Yuri Gagarin was the first man to be sent into space on board a *Vostok* spaceship. The USA sent its first astronaut, Alan Shepard, into space a few months after Gagarin, but the USSR had established a clear lead in the Space Race.

The Earth seen from space.

It's Amazing!

The first two living creatures to survive going into space and re-entering into the Earth's atmosphere were the dogs Belka and Strelka in 1960.

Vostok 1

The spherical *Vostok* spacecraft that took Yuri Gagarin into space was launched from the Baikonur Cosmodrome. The flight lasted 108 minutes. It ended when Gagarin ejected from the capsule. He was 7 km above the ground and had to parachute down to safety.

Sputnik 1

Sputnik I was launched on top of a rocket from the Baikonur Cosmodrome in what is now Kazakhstan on 4 October 1957. The spherical satellite only measured 58.5 cm in diameter. It travelled at 29,000 km/h and broadcast radio signals for 22 days until its transmitter batteries ran out.

A man on the Moon

In May 1961, US president John Kennedy committed the USA to landing a man on the Moon by the end of the decade. The Americans were behind the Soviet Union in the space race, so the Apollo space programme was devised to help them catch up.

The Apollo programme

The Apollo space programme was the most ambitious project any nation had undertaken during peacetime. At its peak, almost half a million people were working for it. Their goal was to design a craft that would carry three human beings to the Moon, 380,000 km away.

Apollo 11 was launched on top of the 111-m-tall, three-stage Saturn V rocket.

Tragic beginnings

The first launch in 1967 was a disaster. The three astronauts were killed when a fire broke out on the launch pad. Subsequent flights put astronauts into orbit around first the Earth and then the Moon, testing the equipment they would need to land on the Moon.

Moon walking

By 1969, the Apollo project was ready. On 16 July, *Apollo 11* blasted off from Cape Kennedy in Florida. Once in Moon orbit, the lunar module *Eagle* separated from the command module, taking Neil Armstrong and Buzz Aldrin down to the surface of the Moon. On 20 July, at 10.56 pm, Armstrong made history by walking on the moon, followed shortly afterwards by Aldrin.

Buzz Aldrin steps down from the *Eagle* on to the Moon.

What Next!

After the success of Apollo 11, five more manned missions landed on the Moon. The last was in 1972. Nobody has been there since.

Timeline

27 January 1967
Apollo 1 catches fire on the launch pad, killing the three astronauts on board

11 October 1968
Apollo 7 makes manned flight around the Earth

21 December 1968
Apollo 8 makes first manned flight around the Moon

20 July 1969
Apollo 11 makes first Moon landing

26 July 1971
Apollo 15 sends a rover vehicle to explore the surface of the Moon

7 December 1972
Apollo 17 makes final Apollo mission

The *Apollo 11* crew

Neil Armstrong (left), Edwin 'Buzz' Aldrin (right) and Michael Collins (centre) were all born in 1930. They trained as military pilots before becoming astronauts, making their first space flights in the Gemini programme in 1966. While the other two astronauts descended to the Moon on board the lunar module *Eagle*, Collins remained in orbit around the Moon on board the Columbia command module.

GLOSSARY AND TIMELINE

Archaeology
The study of the material remains of past civilizations.

Archipelago
Large group of islands.

Arctic Circle
Imaginary line around the North Pole that marks the limit of the region that experiences 24-hour darkness in midwinter. A similar line called the Antarctic Circle surrounds the South Pole.

Astrolabe
Instrument used by sailors to measure the height of the Sun at noon, giving the ship's latitude.

Astronaut
American name for a person who travels in space. The Russian equivalent is a cosmonaut.

c.
Abbreviation for the Latin word circa meaning about. It is used when an exact date is unknown and the date shown is approximate.

Caravan
Company of traders travelling together for safety across a desert or potentially hostile area with a train of pack animals, usually camels or horses.

Caravel
Ocean-going, square-rigged, three-masted ship developed by the Portuguese.

Catamaran
Yacht with two hulls.

Chronometer
Watch designed to be accurate in all climate conditions.

Circumnavigation
Journey right round the world.

Colony
Region or country that is controlled by another country.

Commerce
Trade, or the buying or selling of goods on a large scale, usually for profit.

Continent
One of the seven great landmasses of the world: North and South America, Europe, Africa, Asia, Australasia (Oceania) and Antarctica.

Culture
The way of life of a particular people or country, including their art, literature and music.

---

c.1470BC	Egyptians sail to Punt
c.475BC	Hanno sails down west coast of Africa
c.330BC	Pytheas sails round Britain and visits Thule
c.200BC	Polynesians settle Tahiti
138BC	Zhang Qian travels through central Asia
AD399	Faxian travels from China to India
AD629	Xuanzang travels from China to India
AD921	Ibn Fadlan travels through central Asia
c.1000	Leif Erikson sails to Vinland
1253	William of Rubruck visits the Great Khan
1271	Marco Polo sets out for China
1325	Ibn Battuta sets off from Tangier for Mecca
1405	Zheng He starts the first of his seven voyages
1418	Henry the Navigator founds school at Sagres
1486	Diogo Cão sails to Cape Cross in Namibia
1488	Bartolomeu Dias rounds Cape of Good Hope
1492	Christopher Columbus sails across Atlantic
1497	Vasco da Gama opens up sea route to India; John Cabot sails to Newfoundland
1499	Amerigo Vespucci sails along coast of Brazil
1513	Núñez de Balboa sights the Pacific Ocean
1519	Ferdinand Magellan sets out west from Europe
1521	Hernán Cortés seizes Aztec empire
1522	Delcano completes first circumnavigation

Empire
Many different lands and countries ruled over by one leader.

Equator
Imaginary line around the Earth at an equal distance between the North and South Poles.

Frigate
Medium-sized warship of the 18th and 19th centuries.

Galleon
Large sailing ship used as a warship or merchant ship.

Geology
The study of the solid matter of the Earth, including rocks and soil.

Headwaters
Streams which flow into one another to start a river.

Hydrography
The study of the Earth's oceans, seas and rivers.

Isthmus
Narrow strip of land connecting two larger areas of land.

Junk
Chinese sailing vessel with a flat bottom and square sails.

Ketch
Two-masted sailing vessel.

Knot
A speed of one nautical mile per hour. A nautical mile is equivalent to 1.85 kilometres.

Latitude
The distance north or south of the equator, measured in degrees.

Linguist
Person who studies languages and can usually read and write many different languages.

Log
Detailed record of a ship's voyage, updated every day or sometimes every hour.

Longitude
The distance east or west of a line that runs from the North to the South Pole through Greenwich in England, measured in degrees.

Magnetic South Pole
Place to which all compasses in the southern hemisphere point.

Missionary
A person who travels abroad to convert the local people to his or her religion.

1528	Pánfilo de Narváez explores Florida
1533	Francisco Pizarro seizes Inca empire
1535	Jacques Cartier searches for Northwest Passage
1541	Francis Xavier travels through Asia
1553	Richard Chancellor finds sea route to Russia
1568	Alvaro de Mendaña sails across the Pacific
1577	Francis Drake begins circumnavigation
1594	Willem Barents searches for Northeast Passage
1603	Samuel de Champlain explores Canada
1607	Luis Váez de Torres sails round New Guinea
1610	Henry Hudson discovers the Hudson Strait
1624	Antonio de Andrade crosses the Himalayas
1642	Abel Tasman sails round Australia
1661	Grueber and D'Orville visit Lhasa
1673	Louis Jolliet explores Mississippi
1674	William Dampier begins circumnavigation
1682	Cavelier de La Salle reaches Mississippi delta
1725	Vitus Bering journeys to Siberia
1740	George Anson sets sail around the world
1766	John Byron completes circumnavigation; Louis-Antoine de Bougainville sets out to colonize South Pacific from France
1768	James Cook sets sail for the Pacific
1770	James Bruce discovers the source of the Blue Nile

Monastery
Place of residence of a religious order of monks.

Monohull
Yacht with a single hull.

Mutiny
Rebellion by seamen or soldiers against their commanding officers.

New World
Term used by Europeans to describe North America after they first visited it in the 16th century. Europe, Asia and Africa became known as the Old World.

Nomads
People who move from place to place in search of food, water and land for their animals to graze.

Northern hemisphere
The half of the Earth that lies north of the Equator.

North Pole
Northernmost point of the Earth's axis of rotation, which lies in the Arctic Circle.

Northeast Passage
Route from the Atlantic Ocean round north of Siberia into the Pacific Ocean.

Northwest Passage
Route from the Atlantic Ocean round the north of Canada into the Pacific Ocean.

Oceanography
Study of the world's oceans and their physical, chemical, geological and biological features.

Pack ice
Ice floating on the sea or ocean, which has become packed together in huge sheets, found in the Arctic and Antarctic.

Padrão
Stone cross used by Portuguese navigators to mark their progress down the African coast.

Peninsula
Narrow strip of land surrounded by water on three sides.

Pilgrimage
Journey to a shrine or other sacred place, made by a pilgrim.

Polar
Relating to the North or South Poles.

Polar ice cap
Frozen sheet of ice that covers the area around the North and South Poles.

Press-gang
Group of usually armed men who force civilians to join the army or navy.

Quadrant
Navigation instrument used by sailors to calculate the angle of a star so that they can work out a ship's latitude. The quadrant was replaced in the 18th century by the octant, and then the more accurate sextant.

Schooner
Sailing vessel with at least two masts. All the lower sails on a schooner are rigged from front to back.

Scurvy
Disease caused by a lack of vitamin C, which often used to affect sailors when they did not eat fresh fruit or vegetables on long voyages.

Scuttle
To deliberately sink a ship to stop it from falling into enemy hands.

Silk Road
Ancient trade route linking China through central Asia and the Middle East to the Mediterranean and on to Europe.

Sloop
A single-masted sailing vessel.

Source
The spring or headwaters from which a river begins.

Southern hemisphere
The half of the Earth that lies south of the Equator.

South Pole
Southernmost point of the Earth's axis of rotation, which lies in Antarctica.

Square-rigged
Ship rigged with square or rectangular sails, often hanging from a solid beam.

Storeship
A ship used purely to store supplies for an expedition.

Strait
Narrow channel of water between two seas or oceans.

Trade
The process of buying and selling goods.

Treasure ship
Galleon or other large ship used to carry gold, silver and other precious goods.

Trimaran
Yacht with three hulls, usually with a main hull flanked by two smaller hulls.

Tsar
The hereditary emperor or ruler of Russia. Also spelt czar.

1895	Joshua Slocum sets out on solo voyage around the world
1899	Gertrude Bell starts to explore Middle East
1900	Aurel Stein starts to explore western China
1906	Roald Amundsen navigates Northwest Passage
1909	Peary and Henson reach North Pole
1911	Roald Amundsen reaches South Pole
1927	Freya Stark travels through Arabian desert
1930	Bertram Thomas crosses Empty Quarter; Beebe and Barton make their first descent in the bathysphere in the waters off Bermuda
1943	Jacques Cousteau invents the aqualung
1945	Wilfred Thesiger explores the Empty Quarter
1947	Thor Heyerdahl crosses Pacific on *Kon-Tiki*
1953	Hillary and Tenzing climb Everest
1957	USSR launches first satellite, *Sputnik 1*
1958	Vivian Fuchs crosses Antarctica
1960	*Trieste* descends to bottom of Mariana Trench
1961	Yuri Gagarin is first man in space
1967	Francis Chichester completes first solo, one-stop circumnavigation
1969	Robin Knox-Johnston completes first solo, non-stop circumnavigation; Armstrong and Aldrin walk on the Moon
2008	Francis Joyon sets new solo record of 57 days for solo, nonstop circumnavigation

INDEX

ACKNOWLEDGEMENTS

Artwork supplied by Martin McKenna, Michael Welply and Mike White, and through Linden Artists by Adam Hook, Francis Phillipps and Clive Spong

Cover images:
Front: br Laurie Chamberlain/CORBIS, bc CORBIS, bl Tetra Images/CORBIS, c Bert Leidmann/zefa/CORBIS, tr Morton Beebe/CORBIS, tc Ralph A. Clevenger/CORBIS, tl Matthew McKee; Eye Ubiquitous/CORBIS.
Back: bl Steven Vidler/Eurasia Press/CORBIS, bc Jeremy Horner/CORBIS, tl Historical Picture Archive/CORBIS, tr Douglas Pearson/CORBIS.
Spine: Gordon R. Gainer/CORBIS.

1 Shilo Long/Dreamstime.com, 2-3 Alexander Potapov/Dreamstime.com, 6tr Pilar Echeverria/Dreamstime.com, 6b Bryan Busovicki/istockphoto, 6-7 Martin Brown/Dreamstime.com 7t NASA, 7cr NASA, 7b Burillier 7br Robb Cox/istockphoto.com, 8-9 Keren Su/CORBIS, 10-11 Vladimir Korostyshevskiy/Dreamstime.com, 10t Andrew Kershaw/Dreamstime.com, 10b Michał Kram/Dreamstime.com, 12-13 BishkekRocks, 12b Bettmann/CORBIS, 15t Deborah Benbrook/Dreamstime.com, 15b Matthias Kabel, 17 Werner Forman/CORBIS, 18-19 Simon Gurney/Dreamstime.com, 18b Elena Pokrovskaya/Dreamstime.com, 19b Ryszard Laskowski/Dreamstime.com, 20t Denise Kappa/istockphoto, 21t Erik Torpegaard, 21b Dylan Kereluk/creativecommons.org, 22-23 Olof Ekström, 22 Feng Yu/Dreamstime.com, 23 Darja Vorontsova/Dreamstime.com, 24-25 Kazuyoshi Nomachi/Corbis, 24b Pavel Bortel/Dreamstime.com, 25t Stefanie Van Der Vinden/Dreamstime.com, 26-27 Liu Liqun/Corbis, 26b Nasrulla Adnan/Dreamstime.com, 27t Monika Adamczyk/Dreamstime.com, 28t Bettmann/CORBIS, 29t Hamid Sardar/Corbis, 31t Hulton-Deutsch Collection/CORBIS, 32-33 Robert Churchill/iStockphoto, 33t Christopher Elwell/Dreamstime.com, 34-35 Krause, Johansen/Archivo Iconografico, SA/Corbis, 36-37 Archivo Iconografico, S.A./CORBIS, 36t Corbis, 37t The Art Archive/Corbis, 40 Celso Pupo Rodrigues/Dreamstime.com, 41 Krause, Johansen/Archivo Iconografico, SA/Corbis, 42-43 John Van Hasselt/CORBIS SYGMA, 42b Bettmann/CORBIS , 43t Norbert Speicher/istockphoto, 44 Sascha Dunkhorst/Dreamstime.com, 45t Gianni Dagli Orti/CORBIS, 45b Juan jose Gutierrez barrow/Dreamstime.com, 46t Santa Casa de Misericórdia de Lisboa/ Museu de São Roque, Lisbon, Portugal, 46b Arko Datta/Reuters/Corbis, 47b Keith Yong/Dreamstime.com, 48-49 NASA, 48b Bettmann/CORBIS, 49t PoodlesRock/Corbis, 50b National Maritime Museum, London, 51t Tatiana Edrenkina/Dreamstime.com, 51b Daniel J. Cox/Corbis, 52-53 Shilo Long/Dreamstime.com, 52b Bettmann/CORBIS, 53t Steve Estvanik/Dreamstime.com, 54-55 Adeeb Atwan/Dreamstime.com, 55t Bettmann/CORBIS, 55b George Steinmetz/Corbis, 56t Bettmann/Corbis, 56b Rama/Wikipedia ShareAlike, 57t Nik Wheeler/CORBIS, 59t Valery Shanin/Dreamstime.com, 59b Hulton-Deutsch Collection/CORBIS, 60-61 Pierre Colombel/CORBIS, 62l Bettmann/CORBIS, 63t Tradkelly/Dreamstime.com, 64t Library of Congress, 65t Dmitriy Norov/Dreamstime.com, 66-67 Christopher Howey/Dreamstime.com, 66t Bettmann/CORBIS, 66b David Hughes/Dreamstime.com, 67t John Farmar; Cordaiy Photo Library Ltd./CORBIS, 68-69 Stapleton Collection/Corbis, 68b NASA, 70b Bettmann/CORBIS, 71t Marianne Venegoni/Dreamstime.com, 71b Nina Sosnicka /Dreamstime.com, 71-72 Andrew Buckin/Dreamstime.com, 72b Staffan Widstrand/CORBIS, 73t Diego Barucco/Dreamstime.com, 75t Maureen Plainfield/Dreamstime.com, 75b Michael Nicholson/CORBIS, 76 US Library of Congress, 77t Brian0918/Wikipedia Commons, 78-79 Alexander Potapov/Dreamstime.com, 78b Layne Kennedy/CORBIS, 79b Paul A. Souders/CORBIS, 80-81 Pascaline Daniel/Dreamstime.com, 81t Stapleton Collection/Corbis, 81b Anthony Hathaway/Dreamstime.com, 83 Natalie Fobes, 84-85 Koi88/Dreamstime.com, 85b Asian Art & Archaeology, Inc./CORBIS, 86-87 National Gallery, London/CORBIS, 88-89 Historical Picture Archive/CORBIS, 89 Rodrigo roy a Boncato/Dreamstime.com, 91 Frans Lemmens/zefa/Corbis, 92-93 Joel W. Rogers/CORBIS, 93b Baldwin H. Ward & Kathryn C. Ward/CORBIS, 94t The Robert H. Gore, Jr. Numismatic Collection, 95 Burillier, 96-97 Susinder/Dreamstime.com, 96b Bettmann/CORBIS, 97b Andy Rouse/Corbis, 98b Joe Ho/istockphoto, 99b Dmitriy Murashko/Dreamstime.com, 101 Jeff Goldman/Dreamstime.com, 102-103 Owen Franken/CORBIS, 102b Leonard de Selva/CORBIS, 103t Richard Ling/Wikipedia ShareAlike, 104-105 Alexander Hafemann/istockphoto.com, 104b NOAA, 105t Grigory Kubatyan/Dreamstime.com, 105b Naval Art Collection, Washington, D.C., 107t Michael Maslan Historic Photographs/CORBIS, 108-109 Bettmann/CORBIS, 108t Chichester Archive/PPL, 109t Chichester Archive/PPL, 109b Ted Spiegel/CORBIS, 110-111 MOUSIS FRANCOIS/CORBIS SYGMA, 110b PPL Archive, 111b Brett Atkins/Dreamstime.com 112-113 Darrell Gulin/CORBIS, 116t Bettmann/CORBIS, 117b Sergey Ivanov/Dreamstime.com, 118-119 Charles & Josette Lenars/CORBIS, 119 The Art Archive/Corbis, 120-121 Bryan Busovicki/istockphoto, 120t Bettmann/CORBIS, 120b Carlos Santa Maria | Agency: Dreamstime.com, 121 Håkun Svensson, 123t Tom Bean/CORBIS, 123b Library of Congress, 124-125 Douglas Allen/istockphoto, 125b Burstein Collection/CORBIS, 126t Bettmann/CORBIS, 126b Bettmann/CORBIS, 127t CORBIS, 127b NASA, 128b Karl Bodmer, 129t Scott T. Smith/CORBIS, 130-131 Martin Brown/dreamstime.com, 130b Independence National Historical Park, 131t Smithsonian American Art Museum, 131b Michael Thompson/Dreamstime.com, 133t Library of Congress, 133b Remarsh/Dreamstime.com, 134-135 istockphoto, 135r Mark Kostich/istockphoto, 136-137 Erik Reis/Dreamstime.com, 136t Nikolay Okhitin/Dreamstime.com, 136c The Complete Work of Charles Darwin Online, 136b Bobby Deal/Dreamstime.com, 137b Robyn Mackenzie/Dreamstime.com, 138-139 Ron Sumners/Dreamstime.com, 140b Paul Chinn/San Francisco Chronicle/Corbis, 141t Jose Tejo/Dreamstime.com, 142l Michael C. Rockefeller Memorial Collection, 142-143 Bernard Breton/Dreamstime.com, 145b The Gallery Collection/Corbis, 146-147 Michael Willis/istockphoto, 146l National Archive of Canada, 147t Adam Booth/istockphoto.com, 147b Natural History Museum London, 148-149 Alexander Putaya/Dreamstime.com, 148 Museum of History and Industry/CORBIS, 149t Stapleton Collection/Corbis, 150-151 Jeanne Hatch/istockphoto.com, 150l Oksanaphoto/Dreamstime.com, 151t Martyn Unsworth/istockphoto.com, 152l Pilar Echeverria/Dreamstime.com, 153t Michael C. Rockefeller Memorial Collection, 153b Wieslaw Fila/Dreamstime.com, 155b The Gallery Collection/Corbis, 156-157 Robb Cox/istockphoto.com, 157t Penny Tweedie/Corbis, 158-159 Chris Hellier/CORBIS, 159t Antonela Magzan/Dreamstime.com, 160t John McDouall Stuart Society, 161t John McDouall Stuart Society, 162-163 Kon Tiki Museum, 162l Bettmann/CORBIS, 163t Pcphotos/Dreamstime.com, 163b Margita Braze/Dreamstime.com, 164-165 Vladimir Kindrachov/Dreamstime.com, 166-167 Remi Benali/Corbis, 167t Alan Tobey/istockphoto.com, 169 Christie's Images/CORBIS, 170-171 François De Ribaucourt/Dreamstime.com, 170b Kornelis Bakker/istockphoto.com, 171t Wolfgang Kaehler/CORBIS, 173t Alan Tobey/istockphoto, 174-175 Torleif Svensson/CORBIS, 174t Krause, Johansen/Archivo Iconografico, SA/Corbis, 174b Jacob Eliosoff, 176-177 Michael S. Lewis/CORBIS, 176t Stapleton Collection/Corbis, 177t Luc Sesselle/ Dreamstime.com, 178t Stapleton Collection/Corbis, 179t Klaas Lingbeek- van Kranen/istockphoto.com, 179b Liz Leyden/istockphoto, 180b Hulton archive/istockphoto.com, 182-183 Bettmann/CORBIS, 182b Nik Wheeler/CORBIS, 184t Natalia Siverina/Dreamstime.com, 184br Svetlana Larina/Dreamstime.com, 184-185t Peter Gustafson/Dreamstime.com, 184-185b Elena Schweitzer/Dreamstime.com, 185t Natalia Siverina/Dreamstime.com, 186t Smithsonian Institution, 187t Hulton-Deutsch Collection/CORBIS, 188-189 Philippe Giraud/Goodlook/Corbis, 189t Lindsay Hebberd/CORBIS, 189b Chris Fourie/Dreamstime.com, 190-191 Bernard Breton/Dreamstime.com, 192-193 Tomasz Resiak/istockphoto, 192t US Library of Congress, 192b US Library of Congress, 193t US Library of Congress, 194-195 Stapleton Collection/Corbis, 194t US Library of Congress, 195t US Library of Congress, 196b Bettmann/CORBIS, 197t Ian Stevens, 198t Hulton-Deutsch Collection/CORBIS, 198b Bettmann/Corbis, 200l Underwood & Underwood/CORBIS, 200r US Library of Congress, 201b Morton Beebe/CORBIS, 202l Brad Sauter/Dreamstime.com, 202b Kai Hecker/Dreamstime.com, 203tl Vividpixels/Dreamstime.com, 203tr Kirsty Pargeter/Dreamstime.com, 203r Igor Terekhov/Dreamstime.com, 204t NOAA Photo Library, 205b istockphoto.com, 206-207 Dr. Steve Ross/NOAA, 206b Ralph White/CORBIS, 208-209 Matthias Weinrich/Dreamstime.com, 208b Doxa, 209b Simon Gurney/istockphoto.com, 210-211 Jose Fuente/Dreamstime.com, 210b Bettmann/CORBIS, 211t Peter Hazlett/Dreamstime.com, 211b Robert Churchill/istockphoto, 212-213 NASA, 214l NASA 214-215t NASA, 214-215b NASA